Also by Chris Pilkerton

Underserved: Harnessing the Principles of Lincoln's Vision for Reconstruction for Today's Forgotten Communities

Courses: A Menu for Public Policy with Chef James Beard and Senator J. William Fulbright

PLANDEMIC

Covid, PPP & A Small Business Prescription for the Next Global Economic Crisis

Chris Pilkerton

Post Hill Press

A POST HILL PRESS BOOK
ISBN: 979-8-88845-698-9
ISBN (eBook): 979-8-88845-699-6

Plandemic:
COVID, PPP & A Small Business Prescription for the Next Global Economic Crisis

Cover design by Conroy Accord

This is a work of nonfiction. All people, locations, events, and situations are portrayed to the best of the author's memory.

Post Hill Press
New York • Nashville
posthillpress.com

Published in the United States of America
1 2 3 4 5 6 7 8 9 10

For my father, Dr. A. Raymond Pilkerton Jr., who, with all due respect to Dr. William Osler, is the physician I have learned the most from in my life.

CONTENTS

FOREWORD

In his farewell address to the country, President Ronald Reagan said, "*All great change in America begins at the dinner table.*" In early 2020, families all across the United States watched the same news as the threat of the COVID-19 virus spread throughout the world and onto our shores. Coupled with the tragic news of severe illnesses and deaths, US unemployment rates skyrocketed and stock markets took massive hits.

Under the leadership of President Trump, Secretary Mnuchin and I worked alongside our many White House and Treasury colleagues to develop and implement a financial plan to address the economy in seemingly real time. We all worked night and day in lockstep with congressional leadership to advance the president's goal to protect the health and safety of our citizens and our economy. This led to the passing of the CARES Act, which of course included the establishment of the Paycheck Protection Program. A novel solution to a historic challenge, the purpose of the PPP was to keep workers connected to their companies in order to sustain the economic fabric of our country through this challenging time.

And in the midst of all of these headwinds, the resilience of the American people prevailed. The economic plan kept people employed, supported our small business community, and provided the foundation for the country to not only make it through those dark days, but also be positioned to succeed once they were behind us. The conversation at those dinner tables turned from despair to hope, and we were honored to play a role in that.

While the Trump administration effectively mobilized the herculean effort to address this once-in-a-century pandemic, in hindsight there are always approaches and processes that can be made more effective and efficient. That principle is at the core of innovation and, quite frankly, at the core of the American experience. I am pleased that Chris has conducted this analysis of those days and this program. During the COVID-19 era, the world learned many lessons, but a meaningful review of those experiences in the context of both social and economic circumstances can be of great value to future policymakers. It is nearly impossible to document every detail of those difficult days, but this work provides critical items to consider and discuss should our country be faced with another global pandemic or similar economic crisis.

President Reagan taught us that America should be strong at home and strong abroad. While that was certainly true in the context of our international diplomacy and defense, it may just also apply to a global disease against which the whole world is fighting. And while we can surely benefit from understanding the impacts of approaches taken by other countries, at that moment in time, America led the world—as it always seems to do. We guided the effort to establish a vaccine in record time and navigated our economy through some of the most difficult circumstances it had ever encountered, the ripple effects of which undoubtedly provided great support to the global economy.

To paraphrase the Gipper, America will always be that shining city on the hill, and I believe our response to the pandemic reinforced those immortal words.

Larry Kudlow
Former Director of the US National Economic Council

INTRODUCTION

Medicine is learned by the bedside and not in the classroom. Let not your conceptions of disease come from the words heard in the lecture room or read from the book. See and then reason and compare and control. But see first.

To truly understand the mechanics of any disease, and certainly any pandemic, there must be rigorous scientific diligence into its origins, diagnosis, treatment, complications, and consequences. The professional best positioned to provide such an understanding is most obviously a physician, and the skillset of one physician uniquely situated to offer a critical window into this world is Sir William Osler, MD, often referred to as the Father of Modern Medicine. Dr. Osler was educated in Canada and went on to a diverse study of medical regimens across Europe, including time in London, Berlin, and Vienna, engaging in the study and practice of physiology, pathology, surgery, and neurology.[1] After working as the attending physician at the Montreal General Hospital, he went on to the University of Pennsylvania, serving as both teacher and clinician. Five years later, in 1889, he was asked to establish a clinical program at the newly created Johns Hopkins Hospital and Medical School in Baltimore, Maryland.

1 *The Quotable Osler*, Mark Silverman, T. Jock Murray, and Charles S. Bryan, eds. (American College of Physicians, 2007)

While Dr. Osler provided significant research contributions to the medical field, it was his training model that would go on to become the archetype of clinical education in the United States. In 1891, he published his opus, *The Principles and Practice of Medicine*, which incorporated his strong but not commonly held position that students must engage directly with patients to learn their craft.[2] This book would impact generations of doctors for more than half a century and set the stage for much of modern medical training.[3] He would later serve as a professor at Oxford University and be remembered by a renowned medical historian as "*the greatest physician of our time. He was one of Nature's chosen.*"[4] Not necessarily to draw any historic political comparisons, but one eminent neurosurgeon shared that Dr. Osler "*belongs to medical students of all time, as Lincoln belongs to the common man everywhere...and in whose footsteps any undergraduate may dare to 'hope and dream' that [they] may follow.*"[5]

In 2020, physicians from all around the world who had benefited from Dr. Osler's legacy took on a whole new challenge—a once-in-a-century global pandemic. Early that year, the novel coronavirus was mentioned in the news, but not necessarily

---

2 *The Quotable Osler*, Silverman, Murray, and Bryan. Osler commented to one of this colleagues that they were both lucky to get in as professors as neither would have been admitted as students.

3 *The Quotable Osler*, Silverman, Murray, and Bryan

4 *The Quotable Osler*, Silverman, Murray, and Bryan

5 *The Quotable Osler*, Silverman, Murray, and Bryan. All of this said, Dr. Osler was admittedly not a perfect man. Like many men of his era, he is rumored to have had some antiquated opinions toward women and the medical profession earlier in his career, and while there is no excuse posed here to rebut these or any other allegations against the man himself, his impact on modern medicine is well-documented and very much admired around the globe. See *Sir William Osler: An Encyclopedia*, Charles S. Bryan, ed. (Norman Publishing, 2020)

as the lead story. And while the public were receiving periodic updates of some seemingly geographically limited cases, corporate America began experiencing certain global supply chain disruptions due to quarantines in critical locations within China and elsewhere. This, of course, led to impacts on the delivery of many commercial and consumer goods alike, resulting in downstream effects on reported corporate profits and associated credit and liquidity constraints for large companies.[6] But the impacts of the disease would quickly move from Wall Street to the heart of Main Street.

As the weeks went on, reports of the more commonly used term "COVID-19 virus" became more frequent; and while little was initially known about the origins of the disease or its health impacts, government agencies began to assess worst-case scenarios of fighting widespread contagion of both a health and economic nature. At the time, US interest rates were very low, which created an economic environment positioned to ease some concerns around capital access; but certain companies recognized the economic headwinds that they would soon be facing and planned accordingly, leading to cost-cutting strategies, salary reductions, and the potential for outright layoffs. Nonessential social engagement intentionally lessened across the country to avoid infection, leading to retail customers avoiding all kinds of interactions—whether it be simply exercising at a gym, going out for the evening, or traveling via subway or airplane for work or pleasure. Much of this continued the dam-

6 "The Ignominious Life of the Paycheck Protection Program," Ilya Beylin, *Journal of Legislation and Public Policy*, July 26, 2020; available at SSRN: https://ssrn.com/abstract=3661005 or http://dx.doi.org/10.2139/ssrn.3661005

aging financial impacts on corporate balance sheets and took a toll on energy prices and the global financial markets as well.

Contemporaneously, very large corporations, such as General Motors and Ford, temporarily closed facilities, further signaling the potentially significant nature of a pandemic.[7] Following suit, where possible, small businesses sent their employees to work from home, states and communities went on versions of lockdowns, and US unemployment claims mounted as the stock market lost significant value, as compared to the historic gains of the previous three years.

The federal government sought to weave together a comprehensive health and economic legislative answer to address what would soon become the most significant pandemic the United States had seen in over a century. In late March 2020, at a taxpayer cost of over $2 trillion, the Coronavirus Aid, Relief, and Economic Security (CARES) Act passed Congress and was signed into law by President Donald J. Trump.[8] Coming into the COVID-19 pandemic, the US had approximately thirty-two million small businesses, contributing significantly to the labor market and the nation's gross domestic product. However, the outlook for entrepreneurs during this time was quickly becoming catastrophic. Revenues across the small business sector were plunging, credit possibilities were drying up, workers were being

7 "General Motors, Ford and Fiat Chrysler to Temporarily Close All US Factories Due to the Coronavirus," Phil LeBeau and Noah Higgins-Dunn, CNBC, March 18, 2020, https://www.cnbc.com/2020/03/18/general-motors-ford-and-fiat-chrysler-to-close-all-us-factories-due-to-the-coronavirus-sources-say.html#:~:text=Autos-General%20Motors%2C%20Ford%20and%20Fiat%20Chrysler%20to%20temporarily%20close%20all,factories%20due%20to%20the%20coronavirus&text=The%20Big%20Three%20automakers%20plan,coronavirus%20sweeps%20across%20the%20country

8 "The Ignominious Life of the Paycheck Protection Program," Beylin

laid off, and businesses were preparing to close given the extreme economic pressure of the disease.[9]

While large businesses were under considerable stress as well, given their market capitalization, they had access to systems and resources that small businesses simply did not. And though the CARES Act and subsequent legislation would ultimately provide certain support for these large corporations, small businesses employed almost half of all US workers, and if these small businesses—or in the context of this book, these *patients*—failed, it was feared that conditions could most certainly lead to a major economic slowdown, if not an outright financial calamity.[10]

To mitigate these domestic impacts, the CARES Act created a unique policy package, including something called the Paycheck Protection Program (PPP), which essentially provided forgivable loans to small businesses across the country, generally conditioned on the premise that employers would seek to retain their workers. The CARES Act legislation was over three hundred pages long, but only thirteen pages outlined the parameters of the PPP. The operational package for the PPP was for eligible businesses to engage directly with commercial lenders to receive these funds, and the US Small Business Administration (SBA) would serve in a version of its traditional role as loan guarantor to those lenders, but in this instance, this army of firms would ultimately be reimbursed by the SBA with the appropriations associ-

9 "The $800 Billion Paycheck Protection Program: Where Did the Money Go and Why Did It Go There?" David Autor, David Cho, Leland D. Crane, Mita Goldar, Byron Lutz, Joshua Montes, William B. Peterman, David Ratner, Daniel Villar, and Ahu Yildirmaz, National Bureau of Economic Research, January 2022, https://www.nber.org/system/files/working_papers/w29669/w29669.pdf

10 "The $800 Billion Paycheck Protection Program," Autor et al.

ated with the CARES Act.[11] Over the next eighteen months, this program would skyrocket to nearly $1 trillion of taxpayer-funded support—saving millions of jobs and businesses.[12] This is the story of that time and what the US government—and countries around the world—tried to do to stem the economic waves crashing down on the small business community.

It is widely held that those who do not know history are doomed to repeat it. And much like the plans set forth on the public health topic, this book endeavors to examine the resources developed by government entities to sustain small businesses during the COVID-19 pandemic and seeks to provide a general assessment of what worked and what did not. Recognizing that some of the methods utilized in the US were innovative and unique to this circumstance, this review will broaden to global society and, ultimately, provide a playbook of sorts to apply to potential future pandemics and other significant economic events, disasters, and recessions. As such potentially catastrophic events in the future are deemed almost inevitable by most scientists and experts, the goal is to provide this text as an initial resource for those seeking to utilize best policy practices to support small businesses through these crises.

And who better to take the lead than Dr. Osler? A caregiver who recognized that to tackle any disease and treat any individual, the practitioner must not only have an academic understanding of the ailment but also engage directly with the infected individual to design the most effective and practical treatment to sustain the requisite healing. Much like a physician treating a patient, each

11 "The $800 Billion Paycheck Protection Program," Autor et al.

12 "The $800 Billion Paycheck Protection Program," Autor et al.

chapter will begin with a principle set forth by Dr. Osler as part of his groundbreaking regimen that has served as the foundation to the practice of the modern-day physician. The concept will then be identified and highlighted through an approach that was or could be taken by policymakers in the future as they assess and treat the challenges to small businesses during economic crises.

And so, notwithstanding the overwhelming nature of the task, we embark on this examination under the tutelage of Dr. Osler in his introductory lecture, where he shared, "*Think not of the amount to be accomplished, the difficulties to be overcome....*" In other words, as the editors of *The Quotable Osler* summarized, "*Do first what has to be done.*" [13]

---

13 *The Quotable Osler*, Silverman, Murray, and Bryan

SECTION I

The Disease & The Treatment

CHAPTER ONE

Inevitability of Pandemics, Recessions, and the Early Days of COVID-19

Variability is the law of life, and as no two faces are the same, so no two bodies are alike, and no two individuals react alike and behave alike under the abnormal conditions which we know as disease.

CERTAINLY, ANY LAYPERSON CAN UNDERSTAND Dr. Osler's contention set forth in the above principle, as we all know that even similarly situated people can react very differently to both major and minor illnesses. Whether it be genetics, preexisting health conditions, age, or strength of the disease variant, it stands to reason that symptoms and recommended treatments may differ from person to person. We also know that one of the biggest challenges of preventing, or at least mitigating, the impact of the disease is its ability to modify as it infects its various hosts. While the disease may be clinically treated and a patient may seemingly become asymptomatic, that does not necessarily mean that it or its future mutations have been totally erased. In fact, it may lie dormant, taking some other form or identifying a line of susceptibility that might become vulnerable during the next outbreak. Notwithstanding experience and expertise, humans are not infallible, and as revealed by famed microbiologist Louis Pasteur: "*It is the microbes who will have the last word.*"[1]

In fact, pandemics and economic challenges have inhabited the globe as far back as human history can record. Take, for instance, the Antonine Plague in ancient Rome. Also known as the Plague of Galen, named after the physician who treated many of the cases, this epidemic resulted in nearly two thousand people dying daily, including massive losses to the Roman army. This led to the empire's inability to defend itself from marauders and other enemies invading its borders. And even with the inspirational prose of the Roman leader Marcus Aurelius to encourage his people to be "fearless" in the face of the pandemic, by its conclusion in AD 180, it would ultimately cost the Roman Empire as many as ten million of its countrymen.[2]

The Antonine Plague has been cited as the worst pandemic in the nearly thousand-year history of the Roman Empire. As a leader, Marcus Aurelius spoke of the need for *sympatheia*, the idea that all people are tied together and that humanity suffers

---

1 "Microbes Have the Last Word. A Drastic Re-evaluation of Antimicrobial Treatment Is Needed to Overcome the Threat of Antibiotic-Resistant Bacteria," Julian Davies, *EMBO Reports*, vol. 8, no. 7, July 2007; available at NIH National Library of Medicine: https://www.ncbi.nlm.nih.gov/pmc/articles/PMC1905906/#:~:text=However%2C%20as%20Louis%20Pasteur%20once,no%20antibiotic%20activity%20at%20all

2 *History of Pandemics: The Definitive Guide to Discover the Worst and Deadliest Epidemics and Pandemics That Changed Our World: From the Roman Empire to the Modern Era*, David Anversa (self-published, 2020)

among the shared pain of the world.[3] In a phrase of his own, "*What is bad for the hive is bad for the bee*," he expressed the natural connectivity of this collective experience.[4] In many ways this picture, and perhaps these feelings, became immeasurably more amplified with the daily metrics of infections and deaths scrolling across cable news and social media during the COVID-19 pandemic. However, it would be the thoughtful actions of so many dedicated public and private sector professionals whose contributions would seek to avoid a similar result.

And the Romans were not alone in their experience with pandemics, as the Greeks, too, underwent a very deadly period of disease known as the Plague of Athens around 430 BC.[5] It is estimated that the death toll was as high as one hundred thousand, claiming nearly a quarter of the population of the city.[6] That pandemic rocked rich and poor alike, resulting in massive lawlessness, as homes were invaded and valuables were stolen in order for the vandals to enjoy their spoils before they, too, became victims of the disease.[7] This ultimately led to an increased social role for law enforcement, in part to support the rule of law in future outbreaks.[8] Moving forward quite a few centuries, the more recent Spanish Flu took hold of the world in March 1918. Identified in multiple waves, it is said to have infected approximately half a billion people around the globe, claiming as many as fifty million lives.[9] However, somewhat unique to this tragedy, was that it

---

3 *History of Pandemics: The Definitive Guide*, Anversa

4 *History of Pandemics: The Definitive Guide*, Anversa

5 *History of Pandemics: The Definitive Guide*. Anversa

6 *History of Pandemics: The Definitive Guide*, Anversa

7 *History of Pandemics: The Definitive Guide*, Anversa

8 *History of Pandemics: The Definitive Guide*, Anversa

9 "Spanish Flu," Cleveland Clinic, September 21, 2021, https://my.clevelandclinic.org/health/diseases/21777-spanish-flu

resulted in microbial causes of the disease becoming more readily studied, resulting in many of the advancements around future containments—including that of the COVID-19 virus.[10]

And along with the health impacts of pandemics, the world has seen its fair share of economic contagions. Take, for example, the Dutch tulip crisis of 1637, where a mix of a bubonic plague and overinvestment in financial products associated with the tulip trade decimated Holland and parts of the European economy—it's an instance of the proverbial economic bubble that once again burst in the technology sector after the dot-com boom of the late 1990s into the early 2000s. In fact, the United States has been no stranger to such financial crises, as the 1800s saw land, banking, and railroad panics; the 1900s experienced the 1929 stock market crash; the 1980s observed the rise of junk bonds and their adverse impact on savings and loans; and of course, the 2000s had the earlier-referenced technology bubble burst just a few years before one of the world's worst financial crises in 2008, which would exacerbate the Great Recession.

As many readers will recall, that financial crisis in 2008 stemmed from something of a classic financial panic anchored in a dubious mortgage market that was tied to widely held financial products throughout the banking and securities sectors. This series of events would ultimately take down revered financial institutions like Lehman Brothers and force the acquisition of many well-known banks in an effort to preserve the American, and ultimately, the global economy. While there was significant government intervention to achieve the desired outcome at that time, including a direct infusion of capital into most all of the

10 "Spanish Flu," Cleveland Clinic

major financial institutions, former Treasury Secretary Henry Paulson, Federal Reserve Chair Ben Bernanke, and New York Federal Reserve President Tim Geithner intimated the difficulties of managing these types of circumstances in their book *First Responders*, stating that *"[o]ne lesson for crisis detection is that it's incredibly hard to predict a financial meltdown,"* and *"[i]n the early phase of any crisis, policymakers have to calibrate how forcefully to respond to a situation they don't yet entirely understand."* In retrospect, they felt that "*better preparation could have created better outcomes.*"[11]

And while these types of economic challenges are often inconceivably immense, we must still endeavor to provide for the preparation called for by those who have witnessed it firsthand, which brings us to early 2020. Coming into that fateful year, the United States was enjoying a record economy, which had recently added millions of jobs, with unemployment rates across multiple demographics at historic lows. Since the 2016 presidential election, the economy had been growing at a strong pace and the stock market indices had reached record levels. Household income was climbing, paychecks were growing, many regions of the US enjoyed increased home prices, and home ownership was on the rise as well. But slowly, and then quickly, everything changed.

Over the course of the first few weeks of 2020, there were numerous press stories about a respiratory illness that seemed to have originated in China, but most health officials initially downplayed its global significance, including early comments

11 *First Responders: Inside the U.S. Strategy for Fighting the 2007–2009 Global Financial Crisis*, Ben S. Bernanke, Timothy F. Geithner, Henry M. Paulson, and Nellie Liang, eds. (Yale University Press, 2020)

from global health experts that echoed this position. In late January 2020, the World Health Organization (WHO) signaled the possibility for concern when WHO Director-General Tedros Adhanom Ghebreyesus referred to the illness as "*an emergency in China, but it has not yet become a global health emergency. It may yet become one.*"[12] Dr. Anthony Fauci, then director of the US National Institute of Allergy and Infectious Diseases, publicly shared that the American people should not be overly concerned about the outbreak in China impacting the US population, stating, "*It's a very, very low risk to the United States.... It isn't something the American public needs to worry about or be frightened about.*"[13] Dr. Nancy Messonnier, then director of the National Center for Immunization and Respiratory Diseases at the Centers for Disease Control and Prevention (CDC), followed up by sharing that "*[w]e at CDC don't have clear evidence that patients are infectious before symptom onset, but we are actively investigating that possibility.... We need to be preparing as if this is a pandemic, but I continue to hope that it is not.*" It was a significant comment that was intended to update but seemingly minimize growing public anxiety around a potential widespread community outbreak.[14]

---

12 "On 3/11/20, WHO Declared a Pandemic. These Quotes and Photos Recall That Historic Time," Ari Daniel, National Public Radio, March 10, 2023, https://health.wusf.usf.edu/npr-health/npr-health/2023-03-10/on-3-11-20-who-declared-a-pandemic-these-quotes-and-photos-recall-that-historic-time

13 "Government Health Agency Official: Coronavirus 'Isn't Something the American Public Need to Worry About,'" J. Edward Moreno, The Hill, January 26, 2020, https://thehill.com/homenews/sunday-talk-shows/479939-government-health-agency-official-corona-virus-isnt-something-the/

14 "CDC Official: We're 'Preparing as if This Is a Pandemic,'" Elizabeth Cohen and John Bonfield, CNN, January 26, 2020, https://www.cnn.com/asia/live-news/coronavirus-outbreak-01-27-20-intl-hnk/h_0da030f3c111e8bc2710d089fd9c5b44

At this point, while US officials prepared in the background for what could potentially make its way to its shores, the American public were forced to simply monitor the opinions of the experts and listen to the news reports of lockdowns and temporary public transit system closures in various parts of the world. Early the following week, the WHO revised its guidance when its Executive Director of Health Emergencies Dr. Michael Ryan confirmed that "*[t]he whole world needs to be on alert now. The whole world needs to take action and be ready for any cases that come from the epicenter or other epicenter that becomes established.*"[15] On January 30, the WHO director-general confirmed "*the emergence of a previously unknown pathogen*" which had escalated into an unprecedented virus was, in fact, "*a public health emergency of international concern over the global outbreak of novel coronavirus.*"[16]

Meanwhile, global political leaders sought to mitigate any potential for hysteria. While Chinese President Xi Jinping shared that strict controls in the relevant Chinese geographies were in place in order to limit the outflow of infected individuals, on February 3, United Kingdom's then Prime Minister Boris Johnson noted that any panic around this disease beyond the "*medically rational*" would trigger "*unnecessary*" economic panic.[17] However, as these political comments were being communicated to the global public, Dr. Fauci updated his position that the virus was now "*escalating*" and that "*the number of cases that increase from one day to another is clearly going up in a very steep slope.*"[18]

15 "On 3/11/20, WHO Declared a Pandemic," Daniel

16 "On 3/11/20, WHO Declared a Pandemic," Daniel

17 "Prime Minister Boris Johnson's Speech in Greenwich," February 3, 2020, https://www.gov.uk/government/speeches/pm-speech-in-greenwich-3-february-2020

18 "On 3/11/20, WHO Declared a Pandemic," Daniel

At the same time, US airports began screening for the disease, and on January 28, then US Health and Human Services Secretary Alex Azar went on national television to share that the risk to the American public remained low and that "*Americans should know that this is a potentially very serious public health threat, but, at this point, Americans should not worry for their own safety.... This is a very fast-moving, constantly changing situation.*"[19] As US officials embraced the reality on the ground, by January 30, then CDC Director Dr. Robert Redfield identified that while people within the US had been exposed to the virus, "*based on what we know now, we still believe the immediate risk to the American public is low.*"[20] Over the next few days, US citizens were repatriated from China and quarantined, and on January 31, Secretary Azar declared the outbreak a public health emergency.[21] Just over a week later, the global death toll was over one thousand, and the fifteenth case of the virus was detected in the United States.[22]

By February 11, what had been termed the novel coronavirus had been dubbed "COVID-19" by the WHO director-general, named in part to distinguish it from any previously aligned outbreaks associated with the virus.[23] At a press conference with world leaders, he stated, "*To be honest, a virus is more powerful in creating political, economic, and social upheaval than any terrorist attack.... A virus can have more powerful consequences than any*

19 "Azar: Coronavirus 'A Fast Moving, Constantly Changing Situation,'" Brianna Ehley, Politico, January 28, 2020, https://finance.yahoo.com/news/azar-stops-short-declaring-public-173522024.html

20 "On 3/11/20, WHO Declared a Pandemic," Daniel

21 "COVID-19 Timeline," US Centers for Disease Control and Prevention, https://www.cdc.gov/museum/timeline/covid19.html

22 "COVID-19 Timeline," US Centers for Disease Control and Prevention

23 "COVID-19 Timeline," US Centers for Disease Control and Prevention

terrorist action.... If the world doesn't want to wake up and consider this enemy virus as public enemy number one, I don't think we will learn our lessons."[24] And within two weeks, on February 25, Dr. Messonnier announced that the closing of schools and cancellation of in-person gatherings was soon likely, and "*that disruption to everyday life may be severe.*"[25]

Soon thereafter the warnings about the lower level of risk became less pronounced as cases were identified in different parts of the world, including Iran, New Zealand, and Brazil. The disease that had been believed to be confined to a province within China now had confirmed outbreaks in over one hundred countries; and by March, these nations were going into social lockdown.[26] On March 11, the WHO announced that "*COVID-19 can be characterized as a pandemic.*"[27] On March 13, President Trump declared COVID-19 a national emergency and certain travel bans went into effect.[28] Shortly thereafter, California issued a stay-at-home order, followed by New York, Illinois, Washington, New Jersey, Michigan, and so on.[29]

And all this decisioning was being done among some of the worst economic indicators the country had ever seen. Where there had once been record low unemployment, the totals began to skyrocket. By the end of February and into early March, the

---

24 "On 3/11/20, WHO Declared a Pandemic," Daniel

25 "COVID-19 Timeline," US Centers for Disease Control and Prevention

26 "COVID-19 Timeline," US Centers for Disease Control and Prevention

27 "WHO Director-General's Opening Remarks at the Media Briefing on COVID-19 – March 11, 2020," World Health Organization, https://www.who.int/director-general/speeches/detail/who-director-general-s-opening-remarks-at-the-media-briefing-on-COVID-19---11-march-2020

28 "COVID-19 Timeline," US Centers for Disease Control and Prevention

29 "COVID-19 Timeline," US Centers for Disease Control and Prevention

unemployment claims averaged just about 220,000 a week.[30] By the week ending on March 21, those claims jumped from over 250,000 to almost three million.[31] The next week the claims ballooned to just under six million.[32] By April, unemployment hit 14.7 percent, which was the highest rate since the Great Depression.[33] By comparison, the Great Recession's worst jobs number was approximately 10 percent unemployment, and even that took until October 2009 to reach that mark.[34] Real gross domestic product (GDP), the value of economic output adjusted for price changes, contracted at an annualized rate of 31.4 percent in the second quarter of 2020, whereas the worst decline during the Great Recession was 8.4 percent.[35]

Simultaneously, another major economic indicator combined to demonstrate a disastrous economic outlook. On February 12, the Dow Jones Industrial Average reached a then historic height of 29,551. On March 9, it dropped more than 2,013 points, or almost 8 percent, its single worst drop in history, closing at 23,851.[36] Two days later, the Dow closed at 23,553, down over 20 percent from that February 12 high.[37] Within twenty-four hours, there was another 10 percent drop.[38] By mid-March, it fell to 20,188, top-

30 "Unemployment Insurance Weekly Claims," US Department of Labor Employment and Training Administration report, https://oui.doleta.gov/unemploy/claims.asp

31 "Unemployment Insurance Weekly Claims," US Department of Labor report

32 "Unemployment Insurance Weekly Claims," US Department of Labor report

33 "Has the Paycheck Protection Program Succeeded?" Glenn Hubbard and Michael R. Strain, IZA Institute of Labor Economics, IZA Discussion Paper No. 13808, October 2020, https://docs.iza.org/dp13808.pdf

34 "Has the Paycheck Protection Program Succeeded?" Hubbard and Strain

35 "Has the Paycheck Protection Program Succeeded?" Hubbard and Strain

36 Dow Jones Industrial Average, Federal Reserve Bank of Saint Louis, https://fred.stlouisfed.org/series/DJIA

37 Dow Jones Industrial Average, Federal Reserve Bank of Saint Louis

38 Dow Jones Industrial Average, Federal Reserve Bank of Saint Louis

ping the just-under-13-percent fall of the infamous October 1929 Black Monday stock market crash.[39] All in all, from February 12 to March 15, 2020, the Dow lost a total of 9,362.90 points, which amounted to a 31.7 percent decrease.[40] The markets and investor confidence were in freefall, and something had to be done.

In those early days, the White House National Economic Council (NEC) established an interagency working group to evaluate the expected fiscal impacts and necessary preparations to engage with Congress to determine what the financial structure of a bipartisan multifaceted response to any sizable outbreak could be, all the while seeking to ensure that a presumably unwarranted panic did not spike social and economic alarm.

In 2020, the Democratic Party had a voting majority in the US House of Representatives, and the Republicans had the majority in the US Senate. The Speaker of the House at the time was Nancy Pelosi, a Democrat from California. Along with then House Republican Minority Leader Kevin McCarthy of California, Senate Republican Majority Leader Mitch McConnell from Kentucky, and Senate Democratic Majority Leader Chuck Schumer from New York, this collective group of leadership was anecdotally referred to as the "Four Corners." In all congressional negotiations, members must make numerous decisions on policy goals, gauge viability of legislation, and consider reasonable appropriations and drafting strategies. However, the big ideas almost always need to make it through this group.

From time to time, legislative language might be somewhat vague on certain execution components so that the agency sub-

39 Dow Jones Industrial Average, Federal Reserve Bank of Saint Louis

40 Dow Jones Industrial Average, Federal Reserve Bank of Saint Louis

ject matter experts charged with implementing it can do so by writing specific rules and regulations that provide a clear and efficient framework for everyone affected by the law. Under federal administrative law standards, this process can include proposed rule writings, public notice and comment periods, community listening sessions, and other guidance documents. It can last months or even years. For various reasons, it is almost never done on an expedited basis. However, in the second week of March 2020, in the wake of the largest one-day stock decline since 2008, President Trump began to publicly discuss possible economic actions associated with the immediate circumstances presented by the COVID-19 pandemic. At that time, his referenced ideas included items such as payroll tax cuts and certain legislative initiatives to immediately protect workers impacted by the virus.

To crystalize an approach that would undoubtedly need congressional action, President Trump consulted with Treasury Secretary Steven Mnuchin, NEC Director Larry Kudlow, and Office of Management and Budget (OMB) Acting Director Russ Vought, among many other internal White House leaders. In order to glean relevant private sector expertise, he also took the additional steps of meeting with key Wall Street executives, including the large banks, such as Bank of America, whose CEO Brian Moynihan had made comments early on about an approach, stating that "*[t]he number one thing…to focus on is employees and customers…keep them well, keep them employed and keep them mentally healthy.*"[41]

---

41 "How the $2 Trillion Deal Came Together – and Nearly Fell Apart," John Bresnahan, Marianne Levine, and Andrew Desiderio, Politico, March 26, 2020, https://www.politico.com/news/2020/03/26/inside-the-10-days-to-rescue-the-economy-149718; "'All Hands Should Be on Deck' – Key Quotes from Leaders on the Fight Against COVID-19," World Economic Forum, April 8, 2020, https://www.weforum.org/agenda/2020/04/covid-19-action-call-8-apr/

While many of the stimulus ideas President Trump publicly mentioned were being discussed by numerous economic pundits, certain lawmakers became concerned that tax cuts could become unfairly targeted at particular industries—putting the federal government in the position of picking which businesses could survive the potential economic turmoil. The reality very quickly became that, with almost all but essential workers being put into a position of working from home, much of America would soon become disconnected from in-person interactions. While health measures for testing, vaccine development, and hospital support were ongoing through a historic initiative that would ultimately become known as Operation Warp Speed, the administration needed to determine how various constituencies could be financially supported for a period that was simply unknown at the time. The answer to this seemingly existential question would ultimately require an unprecedented level of government funding and a process to provide unique access to resources for individuals, as well as small and large businesses alike.

In the midst of all of this, under its emergency action authorities, the Federal Reserve announced it would cut the target interest rate to near zero in an effort to prevent a credit crunch and minimize forecasted financial disruptions during these extraordinary circumstances, noting that "*[t]he coronavirus outbreak has harmed communities and disrupted economic activity in many countries, including the United States. Global financial conditions have also been significantly affected.*"[42] Beyond just the sheer size of the potential congressional spending, the financial consequences

42 "Federal Reserve Issues FOMC Statement," Board of Governors of the Federal Reserve System, April 8, 2020, https://www.federalreserve.gov/newsevents/pressreleases/monetary20200315a.htm

of the COVID-19 pandemic presented a unique challenge to economic policymakers. In prior fiscal crises, including during the Great Recession, the core problem triggering the financial decline arose from either within the financial system, such as poorly underwritten mortgages, or other economic policies, such as currency devaluations.

Policymakers had developed well-established tools for these situations to stabilize the financial system to prevent a crisis from producing a sharper and prolonged economic downturn, as seen in how the 1930s banking crisis was handled, which transformed into the Great Depression. The accepted economic strategies to address these types of crises included approaches such as "lender of last resort" lending by the Federal Reserve to both banks through its discount window and non-banks through its emergency lending authority; quantitative easing, where the Federal Reserve purchases substantial amounts of financial assets (treasury securities and non-treasury securities); recapitalization of the banking system by the federal government injecting new capital into the banks; resolution of failed banks to prevent insolvent banks from serving as a drag on economic activity; provision of fiscal stimulus, whereby the federal government substantially increases its spending to spur economic activity; and/or extension of the number of weeks of unemployment insurance in order to support workers who lose their jobs due to the economic downturn.

In short, policymakers had supported the financial system in these ways to stem past panics in the markets to provide time for regulators to address insolvent banks while Congress stimulated the economy with new spending legislation. However, in contrast with these prior economic crises, the COVID-19 pandemic presented these same experts with a threat to the economy that arose from outside of the financial system and the economy. Simply put, given its rarity, the economic impact of a global pandemic was less understood than a banking crisis or other traditional economic emergency. As a result, policymakers had to rely on the assessments of public health officials as to the likely severity of a pandemic and the construct of the prospective public health measures, such as the potential need for lengthy lockdowns, to develop a fulsome economic policy response. And no one had the crystal ball foretelling how long all of this could last.

And of course, at this point, all the decisioning discussed herein was being made in the ever-growing echo chamber of traditional, social, and cable news media. While public health announcements were managed by various government officials, all those analyses were picked apart for hours by media sources and their on-screen experts. Whether traditionally deemed to be conservative or liberal, networks and other media platforms were sharing stories and content from around the country and across the globe as to what could be expected. As the American people were glued to their televisions, computers, and phones for any public health updates, their attention inevitably fell to these reports to inform them of any bit of information that might shed light on what could transpire in their own particular circumstances.

But in those early days, there was not only a lack of clarity but also a kind of mystery around this disease and questions as to whether any such preparation would even be necessary, given its sheer distance from the United States. In fact, as early as

December 2019, journalist Chen Hongxia reported that illnesses had been observed in a Chinese seafood market, citing that the "*scene had been quarantined, and disease prevention and control and medical personnel were conducting prevention and treatment on the spot.*"[43] This story was uploaded in and translated through Google text, with additional language comparing these circumstances to those surrounding the previous outbreaks of viruses SARS-CoV (severe acute respiratory syndrome coronavirus) and MERS-CoV (Middle East respiratory syndrome coronavirus).[44]

Even a passing comparison to these contagions certainly could incubate considerable concern as to what this new virus could grow to become, and within days, pieces of these reports made their way into the Associated Press, the *Boston Globe*, and *Arizona Daily Star*, among others.[45] That said, even in the midst of all of this, any real threat seemed to be contained. As reported by *Vanity Fair*, even though the *New York Times* was holding an editorial conference in Hong Kong shortly thereafter, while "*[t]he discovery of a novel coronavirus was big news…it didn't even register on the list of major themes that editors and reporters tossed out during the meeting as coverage targets for the coming year.*" As *New York Times* reporter Sui-Lee Wee described, "*Everyone just moved on…. The main themes were climate change, demographics, gender.*"[46]

But ultimately, these stories became much more widely reported and prioritized, and epidemic comparisons were shared

---

43 "'I've Just Been Swept Up in This Wave': How the Earliest COVID Coverage Shaped Our World," Joe Pompeo, *Vanity Fair*, December 27, 2021, https://www.vanityfair.com/news/2021/12/how-the-earliest-covid-coverage-shaped-our-world

44 "I've Just Been Swept Up in This Wave," Pompeo

45 "I've Just Been Swept Up in This Wave," Pompeo

46 "I've Just Been Swept Up in This Wave," Pompeo

throughout mainstream and social media. And as cases began to spread, global experts shared their thoughts on the outlook. As reported by CNN, the United Kingdom's Chief Medical Officer Chris Whitty stated that "*the probability of having a vaccine or treatment 'anytime in the next calendar year' is 'incredibly small.'*"[47] This statement and much of the ongoing media coverage fueled the public concern over what impact this pandemic could ultimately have on the daily life of all Americans and the potential for massive economic fallout.[48] Regardless of how or where this information was consumed, public officials continued to face headwinds in ensuring that accurate information was properly disseminated and that the associated analyses were commensurate with public health risks. This, in turn, impacted the speed of the policymaking-response process as the architecture of the legislative proposals endeavored to capture the views of all the various constituencies—on one of the most consequential timelines in the nation's history.

So, on the evening of March 16, 2020, Secretary Mnuchin, NEC Director Kudlow, Acting OMB Director Vought, and White House Legislative Affairs Director Eric Ueland met with Republican Senate leadership, sharing that it was the position of the president that the US economy was going to require significant stimulus in a uniquely expedited fashion, possibly leading

---

47 "I've Just Been Swept Up in This Wave," Pompeo

48 "Why Is All COVID-19 Bad News?" Bruce Sacerdote, Ranjan Sehgal, and Molly Cook, National Bureau of Economic Research, November 2020, https://www.nber.org/papers/w28110; "Perspectives on U.S. Media Coverage of the COVID-19 Pandemic," Guillaume Vandenbroucke, *Regional Economist*, November 23, 2021, https://www.stlouisfed.org/publications/regional-economist/fourth-quarter-2021/perspectives-us-media-coverage-covid19-pandemic#:~:text=KEY%20TAKEAWAYS,tone%20increased%20during%20the%20pandemic

to one of the largest spending bills in US history.[49] Public reports indicate that despite this massive need, congressional negotiations among the Four Corners did not begin smoothly.[50] Externally, congresspeople criticized each other for "*playing politics*" during this dubious period; and notwithstanding public consternation and countless drafts of legislative language, the far-ranging health and economic impacts of the COVID-19 virus became more dire with every passing day.[51]

Reports demonstrate that the priorities on the Republican side included small business aid, loans to distressed industries, direct payments to families, and substantive funding for an appropriate medical response; while Senator Schumer and the Democrats pushed for robust unemployment insurance initiatives, the close monitoring of any corporate loans, funding for states to help offset lost tax revenues, and congressional oversight for certain unique funding authority provided directly to the Treasury Department to support economic stabilization.[52] But still the bill could not come fast enough. Unemployment was rising quickly, businesses were shuttering, and Senate Small Business and Entrepreneurship Committee Chair Senator Marco Rubio, a Republican from Florida, bluntly warned of the immediate need for action, stating, "*What's this country going to look like two weeks from now? Just look how much it has changed in 10 days. Imagine another five. What we're dealing with here is not some ordinary ideological debate during ordinary times or even during an economic downturn. It is a catastrophic collapse of the economy via government fiat.*"[53]

---

49 "How the $2 Trillion Deal Came Together," Bresnahan, Levine, and Desiderio

50 "How the $2 Trillion Deal Came Together," Bresnahan, Levine, and Desiderio

51 "How the $2 Trillion Deal Came Together," Bresnahan, Levine, and Desiderio

52 "How the $2 Trillion Deal Came Together," Bresnahan, Levine, and Desiderio

53 "How the $2 Trillion Deal Came Together," Bresnahan, Levine, and Desiderio

In order to advance the effort, Senator McConnell established four bipartisan task forces to work through the issues so that the legislation could be finalized under an accelerated timetable. Focusing on the open items of unemployment insurance, small business loans, support for hospitals, and funds for distressed communities, Republicans and Democrats worked out of the Senate Finance Committee rooms in the Dirksen Building on Capitol Hill.[54] But even with a dark cloud looming, negotiations seemed to stall from time to time, once again placing Senator Rubio in the position to openly advocate for a solution. "*We're now one day, one hour, one diagnosis away from a significant percentage of the Senate being quarantined and being unable to act. What happens if 20 people get knocked out into a quarantine, or 30? Suddenly you have problems bringing people together to actually pass something, to function, given our current rules.*"[55]

In recognition of this urgency, Republicans introduced a bill, noting that while some of the language would need negotiation, it could serve as a foundation for the ultimate legislation. However, it has been reported that Speaker Pelosi informed Senator McConnell that the House Democrats would introduce their own bill, and that the Senate Democrats were positioned to filibuster the Republican legislation, thereby creating a procedural roadblock to its passage.[56] Versions of what exactly occurred within those halls vary at this point in the process, but Senator Chris Coons, a Democrat from Delaware who sat on the Senate Small Business Committee, noted that at that time, "*[t]he Republicans kind of pulled back from the working groups. They started writ-*

54 "How the $2 Trillion Deal Came Together," Bresnahan, Levine, and Desiderio

55 "How the $2 Trillion Deal Came Together," Bresnahan, Levine, and Desiderio

56 "How the $2 Trillion Deal Came Together," Bresnahan, Levine, and Desiderio

ing language that wasn't broadly shared with Democrats and by Saturday night there was real alarm about where is this all going."[57]

With daily unemployment growing to a point that some believed could challenge Great Depression levels, a panoply of policy options continued to be debated.[58] But in the midst of political barbs and finger pointing, just before 2 a.m. on Wednesday, March 25, a legislative deal was announced. Ultimately, much of the negotiation credit went to Secretary Mnuchin and Director Kudlow as the president's chief negotiators, working alongside Senator Schumer, who stated, "*We packed months of legislative process into five days*."[59]

Some of the anticipated economic responses were textbook in nature. The Federal Reserve would be a key player to ensure that the markets had sufficient liquidity, and existing social safety nets would be strengthened where necessary.[60] While most larger businesses would likely be able to rely on traditional lending, the approach for small and some medium-sized businesses was not necessarily as clear from the beginning. At this point, traditional debt was considered to potentially be too overwhelming for their sensitive balance sheets, most of which could likely only withstand a few weeks of limited to no revenue. And equity injections were just not feasible given the differing sizes and industrial variety of these firms. The final decision was to support a mechanism that would allow for continuity and avoid a chain reaction of business failures, all while preserving employment relationships in the wake of lockdown orders.[61]

---

57 "How the $2 Trillion Deal Came Together," Bresnahan, Levine, and Desiderio

58 "How the $2 Trillion Deal Came Together," Bresnahan, Levine, and Desiderio

59 "How the $2 Trillion Deal Came Together," Bresnahan, Levine, and Desiderio

60 "Has the Paycheck Protection Program Succeeded?" Hubbard and Strain

61 "Has the Paycheck Protection Program Succeeded?" Hubbard and Strain

With employees at small businesses accounting for nearly half of the private sector workforce, bankruptcies and outright closures would have led to overnight calamity for the labor market. If firms would have ultimately failed under traditional market conditions, then they would do so after the program was implemented, but keeping workers paid in the interim would allow for the economic impacts of the pandemic to be mitigated as the identified public health measures took effect.

With the guiding principles of being "*timely, targeted, and temporary*," on March 26, the US Congress passed a remarkable $2.2 trillion stimulus bill called the Coronavirus Aid, Relief, and Economic Security (CARES) Act.[62] To date, it is the largest stand-alone financial rescue package in history, and included the following: $300 billion in direct cash payments to Americans earning less than $99,000 per year ($3,400 for a typical family of four); approximately $350 billion in job retention loans for small businesses with loan forgiveness available for businesses that continued paying their workers (Paycheck Protection Program); $250 billion in expanded unemployment benefits; $500 billion of potential loan capital access for hard-hit industries; over $100 billion to support medical preparedness; $45 billion for the Disaster Relief Fund supporting localities; and $27 billion for the development of vaccines, therapies, and other public health response efforts, including $16 billion to build up the Strategic National Stockpile with critical supplies.[63]

62 "The Job Preservation Effects of Paycheck Protection Program Loans," Michael Faulkender, Robert Jackman, and Stephen Miran, *Social Science Research*, February 15, 2023; available at SSRN: https://papers.ssrn.com/sol3/papers.cfm?abstract_id=3767509

63 "Remarks by President Trump at Signing of H.R. 748, The CARES Act," The White House, March 27, 2020, https://trumpwhitehouse.archives.gov/

But that was just the start. This massive amount of money had to get from the US Treasury into the hands of the American people and had to do so in record time. Now, President Trump, the White House team, Secretary Mnuchin, and the other critical leaders across the executive agencies had to figure out just how to do that. Recognizing that there would be gaps in the process, administration leaders posited that in order to advance things as quickly as possible, the process would need to be built on an existing government infrastructure—namely the distribution capabilities of the US Small Business Administration.[64] While the SBA had always been an important agency in supporting areas of the country impacted by disasters like hurricanes and wildfires, and even in the unique circumstances of September 11, 2001, and the Great Recession; some critics were concerned that the novelty of the PPP approach was too dissimilar to SBA's traditional lending programs and expertise. And the perception of that distinctiveness was legitimate. While components of the plan resembled classic economic stimulus, other pieces were developed as part of the unique circumstances that accounted for the fact that this crisis did not reflect any significant labor or capital reallocation that could be surmounted by mere fiscal intervention. [65] Based on the guidance from public health officials, economic leaders took these steps in light of the need to keep workers economically viable while they sought to "*flatten the curve*" of infection through various public safety protocols and stay-at-home advisories.

---

briefings-statements/remarks-president-trump-signing-h-r-748-cares-act/

64 "The Job Preservation Effects of Paycheck Protection Program Loans," Faulkender, Jackman, and Miran

65 "The Job Preservation Effects of Paycheck Protection Program Loans," Faulkender, Jackman, and Miran

With speed being the most critical factor to limit potential economic contagion, the process understandably had to be designed somewhat on the fly. Stakeholder guidance needed to be drafted and distributed to lenders and businesses. Cities needed to be positioned to provide support to their impacted communities. The White House, Treasury Department, and SBA communication teams had to address changes and discrepancies in guidance in real time and engage almost hourly with friendly and hostile media alike to distribute timely information. National trade associations were positioned to openly support and publicly criticize plans and approaches as directed by their constituencies. And amid a sea of agency employees no longer able to work from their offices, the massive machinery of the federal government was being put to a generational test.

CHAPTER TWO

The Paycheck Protection Program

Medicine is a science of uncertainty and the art of probability.

NOTWITHSTANDING TRUSTED TREATMENTS AND COUNTLESS hours of diagnostic experience, it would seem reasonable that at certain points in their careers, physicians play the odds when it comes to their assessment of a patient. That is not to take away anything from their professional analyses, training, and experience, but no individual is clairvoyant when it comes to the depths of the human body and all the possible illnesses which may impact it. In most circumstances, physicians make very informed and rational decisions to alleviate their patients of disease and discomfort. But of course, there is also the world of experimentation that requires the use of cutting-edge technologies, novel drug treatments, and associated testing to determine whether any remedy is effective and safe for the general population.

And due to the costs of the research and development, often these treatments are reserved for the very significant diseases that impact so many people across the globe. Think of investigational treatments for diabetes, cancer, Alzheimer's, and the like. And this is understandably a critical part of medicine—probing, testing, and pushing to the extremes in the laboratory, so that humanity can ultimately share in the benefit of this work. Of course, this is almost always a very long process that must account for significant trial and error, safety optimization, and a list of countless other concerns. And even when these types of treatments leave the lab, have undergone rigorous studies to prove their efficacy, and are deemed to be commercially viable, the appropriate regulatory bodies must approve their mass distribution.

But what about when that time in the laboratory just isn't available? What about the situations when, if the disease is not treated immediately, the available evidence points to the most negative consequence imaginable—not just for one patient but for thousands or even millions of people? In these circumstances, the decision-makers may look to the guidance of perhaps the most famous doctor in all of human history, the Greek physician Hippocrates, who shared, "*Extreme remedies are very appropriate for extreme diseases*." While the true impacts of mandated or encouraged social lockdowns during the COVID-19 pandemic are still being debated in the public health and policy communities, the reality is that in this circumstance, those instances led to the closing of many businesses, and by the projections of the International Monetary Fund, if handled improperly, could have led to many trillions of dollars in global losses.[1]

1 "Pandemic Economics," R. Agarwal R. and G. Gopinath, International Monetary Fund, *Finance & Development*, December 2021, https://www.imf.org/en/Publications/fandd/issues/2021/12/Pandemic-Economics-Agarwal-Gopinath#:~:text=against%20the%20virus.-,If%20COVID-19%2D19%20were%20to%20have%20a%20prolonged%20impact%2C%20we,several%20million%20more%20lives%20lost

Therefore, the question became this: whether a combination of Hippocrates' contention about extreme remedies and Dr. Osler's position on the use of viable probabilities in treatment could be a reasonable methodology to treat substantial economic crises and massive unemployment. Without the benefit of hindsight that allows for nuanced criticism of the remedies provided, most stakeholders from both the public and private sectors seem to agree that the approach undertaken by the federal government—namely the PPP—was rational under these unique circumstances. Even politics can take a back seat to a real-time assessment of such an overwhelming dilemma. Just ask then Democratic ranking member of the US Senate Small Business Committee Ben Cardin, who shared that "*Congress has a duty to ensure that America's 30 million small businesses, and the 60 million people they employ, are not forced to bear the financial costs of keeping our communities safe on their own.*"[2] Then compare his words to those of his Republican counterpart Senator Rubio, who stated, "*As we fight this public health crisis, the most important thing that we can do for our nation's small businesses and their employees is to provide some certainty—certainty to businesses that they can keep their employees, certainty to employees that they can remain on the payroll and certainty that the connection between employer and employee will remain intact after this crisis passes.*"[3] Or perhaps even ask the CEO of one of America's largest banks charged with distributing the funds, Bank

2 "Cardin, Bipartisan Senate Task Force Secure $377 Billion for Small Businesses," US Senate Committee on Small Business & Entrepreneurship, press release, March 25, 2020, https://www.cardin.senate.gov/press-releases/cardin-bipartisan-senate-task-force-secure-377-billion-for-small-businesses/

3 "ICYMI: Rubio: New Paycheck Protection Program Offers Real Relief for Small Business," US Senator Marco Rubio, press release, March 31, 2020, https://www.rubio.senate.gov/icymi-rubio-new-paycheck-protection-program-offers-real-relief-for-small-business/

of America's Brian Moynihan, who declared that "*[i]t's clear that between Congress, the administration and the American people, we need to get all these funded and not make this a foot race. Just get the work done.*"[4]

That work began at the headquarters of the US Small Business Administration, located just a few blocks from the US Capitol Building, at 403 Third Street, SW, Washington, DC 20416. Although this agency stood at the epicenter of the PPP, only a handful of people physically remained within the walls of the SBA's headquarters, as thousands of its employees around the country had been directed to leave their offices and conduct this work from their homes. In fact, during those early days, the agency lost a colleague to complications from the disease, yet another tragic reminder of the dangers the country was facing and the importance of its efforts. And in the midst of all of this, while still very much connected in this new work-from-home paradigm, the entire staff functioned tirelessly around the clock to operationalize funding processes, craft and draft emergency rules and procedures, and communicate to countless lenders, potential borrowers, and so many other stakeholders. Then SBA Administrator Jovita Carranza, who had held the position of US Treasurer just prior to her appointment, had existing relationships with the key senior Treasury officials who were involved in the congressional negotiations of the CARES Act and were the primary drafters of much of this work. That was of significant benefit to the agency as this group too was in their offices

4 "Bank of America CEO Calls for Congress to 'Fully Fund' Small Business Loan Program: 'Just Get the Work Done,'" Jesse Pound, CNBC, April 26, 2020, https://www.cnbc.com/2020/04/26/coronavirus-bank-of-america-ceo-calls-for-congress-to-fully-fund-ppp.html

working closely with the SBA staff as they all prepared to launch this historic program. With all the same health fears and challenges that so many other in-person workers were facing for both themselves and their families, these public servants worked diligently alongside key industry partners to perform for the American people.[5]

Anecdotally, with so many restaurants closed, the SBA team relied on "*Costco runs*," subsisting on "*coffee, candy, and chips*" to maintain the energy to complete the seemingly 24/7 all-consuming task at hand.[6] Ultimately, the PPP guidelines were finalized and made public on the evening of April 2, the night before the program went live.[7] Notwithstanding their recognition that the rollout was going to have challenges that next morning, all the SBA staff and their Treasury partners could do was wait and address issues as they arose—and they did. In the wake of this rollout, public criticisms came from both the private sector and the media, and staff continued to update the White House, Congress, and other stakeholders in real time.[8] That first day, the state of Montana led the country with over $150 million distributed via 416 loans, and the national day one total of PPP lending was approximately $5.5 billion made through over one thousand lenders.[9] Over the course of the next few weeks, that amount of lending would reach $500 billion; and within a

5 "After 1 Year of PPP, a Former SBA Official on the 'Herculean' Effort Getting the $750 Billion Program Off the Ground," Diana Ransom, *Inc.*, April 9, 2021, https://www.inc.com/diana-ransom/PPP-bill-briggs-paycheck-protection-program-small-business-administration.html

6 "After 1 Year of PPP," Ransom

7 "After 1 Year of PPP," Ransom

8 "After 1 Year of PPP," Ransom

9 "After 1 Year of PPP," Ransom

year, approximately nine million PPP loans would be made, totaling more than three-quarters of $1 trillion.[10] While criticisms would undoubtedly follow, as one small business put it, "*We are in a better place today because of the PPP.*"[11]

But to be clear, this process was by no means perfect. With a mandate for speed, many knew that there would be challenges in the approach set forth by the federal government. In fact, even Senator Rubio shared early on that "*[n]o one's ever done one of these before. There's not a banker in America that's ever given out a PPP loan until Friday. There isn't anybody at the SBA that's ever authorized a PPP loan until Friday. This is not the same as a pre-existing system that isn't working well. This is completely brand new and built—in six days.*"[12] Time would show cracks in the process, as the federal government was criticized for incomplete guidance and miscommunication, and banks were accused of client favoritism and program mismanagement.[13] But all of this was done under the severe reality that by May 23, there were reports of over 1.6 million COVID-19 virus infections across the country with approximately

10 "After 1 Year of PPP," Ransom

11 Testimony of Robert J. Barnes, President and CEO of Priority One Bank, on behalf of the Independent Community Bankers of America, before the US House Committee on Small Business Subcommittee on Oversight, Investigations and Regulations hearing on "An Empirical Review of the Paycheck Protection Program," March 16, 2022; available at ICBA.org: https://www.icba.org/docs/default-source/icba/advocacy-documents/testimony/testimony-on-sba-and-ppp.pdf?sfvrsn=d3c91917_0

12 "A Stampede: Marco Rubio Says Non-Stop Demand for Small Business Rescue Program Is Straining Capacity," Ledyard King, *USA Today*, April 7, 2020, https://www.usatoday.com/story/news/politics/2020/04/07/marco-rubio-small-business-panel-chairman-says-loan-program-improving/2965565001/

13 "Did Banks Play Favorites in PPP or Were They Just Being Prudent?" Neil Haggerty and John Reosti, *American Banker*, April 27, 2020, https://www.americanbanker.com/news/did-banks-play-favorites-in-PPP-or-were-they-just-being-prudent

one hundred thousand people who had succumbed to the disease, millions upon millions of initial unemployment claims, and economic reports that established a potential 33 percent economic contraction for the second quarter of 2020.[14]

So, what were the actual components of the PPP? The initial amount of funding that was authorized for the PPP was approximately $350 billion, allowing eligible small businesses to seek up to ten weeks of annualized salary coverage not to exceed $100,000.[15] Those funds were to be received by the businesses via application to eligible private-sector lenders, which essentially meant anyone that had access to the SBA's electronic transmission system, also known as E-Tran. This ultimately included over five thousand active lenders, as compared to less than half of that for any traditional SBA lending year. This group was made up of banks, credit unions, minority development institutions, community development financial institutions, financial technology firms, farm credit organizations, and other nonbank lenders that were required to make the loan within ten days of borrower approval. In a modification of the agency's flagship 7(a) small business lending program, if the business met its rule-based obligations and submitted the revised short form paperwork application and the evidence of its payroll, mortgage interest, utilities, and rent (all of which fell under

14 "The Early Impact of COVID-19 on Local Commerce: Changes in Spending Across Neighborhoods and Online," JPMorgan Chase Institute, June 2020, https://www.jpmorganchase.com/institute/all-topics/community-development/early-impact-covid-19-local-commerce; "Funding Crises: An Empirical Study of the Paycheck Protection Program," William A. Birdthistle and Joshua Silver, *Buffalo Law Review*, vol. 69, no. 5, 2021, https://digitalcommons.law.buffalo.edu/buffalolawreview/vol69/iss5/5/; and "May 22 Coronavirus News," CNN, Jessie Yeung, Adam Renton, Melissa Macaya, and Fernando Alfonso III, https://www.cnn.com/world/live-news/coronavirus-pandemic-05-22-20-intl/index.html

15 "Paycheck Protection Program (PPP) Information Sheet: Borrowers," https://home.treasury.gov/system/files/136/PPP--Fact-Sheet.pdf

approved uses for a portion of the funds), the loan would be fully forgiven by the lender that would receive its payment directly from the SBA to cover the cost and fees associated with the PPP loan.[16]

Generally speaking, for an applicant to initially be eligible for a PPP loan, it had to be a small business or a certain comparably sized nonprofit under the five-hundred-employee standard and provide payroll reports/tax filings supporting its claim, including a requirement to certify that "*current economic uncertainty makes this loan request necessary to support the ongoing operations of the applicant*."[17] Borrowers did not have to provide collateral or personal guarantees and could qualify for two and a half times their monthly payroll, with a limit of $10 million. Although the initial eligibility standards for the borrowers have been criticized as confusing and somewhat inconsistent, the general conditions were that a loan would be forgiven if the business spent 75 percent of the funds on payroll for the covered period of up to eight

---

16 "*The fees paid to financial institutions that administered the program also had a significant subsidy element. At disbursement, the program paid lenders 5% of the principal for loans under $350,000, 3% for loans between $350,000 and $2 million and 1% for loans over $2 million. Based on the minimal screening requirements, the absence of servicing obligations, the 100% credit guarantee, and federal funding support, we estimate that actual costs to lenders were considerably less than what they were paid. Assuming actual fixed costs of 2% for loans up to $350,000, 0.75% for loans between $350,000 and $2 million, and 0.25% for loans over $2 million, and based on the distribution of realized loan sizes, the subsidies to financial institutions totalled $19.5 billion, a 2.4 percent lender subsidy element.*" (From "Evaluating the Costs of Government Credit Support during the COVID-19: International Evidence," Gee Hee Hong and Deborah Lucas, International Monetary Fund, January 27, 2023, https://www.imf.org/en/Publications/WP/Issues/2023/01/27/Evaluating-the-Costs-of-Government-Credit-Support-Programs-during-COVID-19-International-528660.)

17 "Paycheck Protection Program Loans, Frequently Asked Questions," US Small Business Administration fact sheet, April 26, 2020, https://www.sba.gov/sites/default/files/2023-03/Paycheck-Protection-Program-Frequently-Asked-Questions_04%2026%2020.pdf

weeks. (This would ultimately drop to 60 percent of payroll to account for payment of more operational business expenses, as well as a twenty-four-week covered period for forgiveness.)[18]

On the lenders' end, these loans would have a two-year maturity (ultimately extended to five years) and would carry no weight on their capital requirements. Once the borrower application was submitted to the SBA by the lender, it would receive an identified loan number and ultimately provide the borrower's use of funds paperwork for that covered period.[19] Assuming the borrower documentation met the threshold amounts, the entirety of the loan would be forgiven.[20] This concept of it being a "forgivable loan" was intentional from the outset of the program; however, loans that did not meet the designated standards were deemed to be repayable by the borrower at a 1 percent interest rate.[21] The significant financial focus of the legislative policy was, of course, to maintain or quickly rehire workers as needed, but other related

---

18 "The $800 Billion Paycheck Protection Program: Where Did the Money Go and Why Did It Go There?" David Autor, David Cho, Leland D. Crane, Mita Goldar, Byron Lutz, Joshua Montes, William B. Peterman, David Ratner, Daniel Villar, and Ahu Yildirmaz, National Bureau of Economic Research, January 2022, https://www.nber.org/system/files/working_papers/w29669/w29669.pdf, also noting: *"If these criteria were not met, SBA offered alternative routes to forgiveness. Businesses could exercise a "safe harbor" option to meet the employment and wage criteria by restoring their fulltime equivalent employment and wage rates to their pre-COVID-19 level by the end of 2020 (or by the end of the covered period for loans issued in 2021). This safe harbor provision made the employment criteria far less onerous. Moreover, if a firm did not meet all criteria, loan forgiveness could be partial."*

19 "The $800 Billion Paycheck Protection Program," Autor et al.

20 "The Job Preservation Effects of Paycheck Protection Program Loans," Michael Faulkender, Robert Jackman, and Stephen Miran, *Social Science Research*, February 15, 2023; available at SSRN: https://ssrn.com/abstract=3767509 or http://dx.doi.org/10.2139/ssrn.3767509, noting that the 8 weeks would go to 24 weeks and the 75% would go to 60% later in the life of the PPP.

21 "The Job Preservation Effects of Paycheck Protection Program Loans," Faulkender, Jackman, and Miran

components of the CARES Act allowed for certain debt relief for existing SBA borrowers, paid leave for government contractors, and support for various business counseling resources.[22]

22 A description of the full small business provisions in the initial economic stimulus in the CARES Act follows: Paycheck Protection Program: *The stimulus includes nearly $350 billion in funding for a provision to create a Paycheck Protection Program (PPP) that will provide small businesses and other entities with zero-fee loans of up to $10 million. Up to 8 weeks of average payroll and other costs will be forgiven if the business retains its employees and their salary levels. Principal and interest is deferred for up to a year and all borrower fees are waived. This temporary emergency assistance through the U.S. Small Business Administration (SBA) and the Department of Treasury can be used in coordination with other COVID-19-financing assistance established in the bill or any other existing SBA loan program. The bill requires the SBA Administrator to set a cap on how much a bank can earn to process loan applications and prioritize underserved borrowers, including those in rural communities, minorities, women and veterans.*

Debt Relief for Existing and New SBA Borrowers: The stimulus includes $17 billion in funding for a provision to provide immediate relief to small businesses with standard SBA 7(a), 504, or microloans. Under this provision, SBA will cover all loan payments for existing SBA borrowers, including principal, interest, and fees, for six months. This relief will also be available to new borrowers who take out an SBA loan within six months after the President signs the bill. The measure also encourages banks to provide further relief to small business borrowers by allowing them to extend the duration of existing loans beyond existing limits; and enables small business lenders to assist more new and existing borrowers by providing a temporary extension on certain reporting requirements. While SBA borrowers are receiving the six months debt relief, they may apply for a PPP loan that provides capital to keep their employees on the job. The six months of SBA payment relief may not be applied to payments on PPP loans. The stimulus also includes a permanent fix that allows SBA to waive fees for veterans and their spouses in the 7(a) Express Loan Program, regardless of the President's budget. Under current law, SBA may only waive fees on 7(a) Express loans to veterans when the President's budget does not project a cost above zero for the overall 7(a) loan program.

Paid Leave for Government Contractors: The stimulus includes a provision that provides paid leave for employees working on small business contracts with the federal government. The measure allows agencies to modify the terms of a contract to reimburse small business contractors for the cost of providing paid leave, including sick leave, to employees or subcontractors unable to perform work on-site due to a facility closure and cannot telework.

Resources for Business Counseling Services: Many large companies are struggling to respond to the unprecedented economic disruption our nation is facing, so small businesses that have even fewer resources to dedicate to navigating the economic impacts of COVID-19 must have access to reliable counseling and mentorship services. The stimulus provides $275 million in grants to the nation's network of

As has been demonstrated in so many other national crises, the country undoubtedly experienced a sense of patriotism, community, or perhaps even embraced Marcus Aurelius' concept of *sympatheia* during this time; however, the practical nature of the PPP needed to ensure that lenders had a financial incentive to participate in this program. With that in mind, lenders were permitted to receive fees associated with the loans. For loans under $350,000, they received a 5 percent fee; for loans that were $350,000 to $2 million, they received 3 percent; and for anything greater than $2 million, a 1 percent fee.[23] While the intention was to set the rate as low as possible, this was seen as a requirement so that participants could at least cover the internal cost of setup and delivery of this novel program. Any unforgiven portion of the loan would continue to carry the interest rate to the borrower, but the lender would receive the full SBA guarantee.[24]

That first tranche of PPP funds was exhausted very quickly—in just under two weeks—and for the many borrowers seeking access to the program, an additional amount of $310 billion was approved by Congress in late April 2020 as part of the Paycheck

---

Small Business Development Centers (SBDCs) and Women's Business Centers (WBCs), as well as the Minority Business Development Agency's Business Centers (MBDCs), to provide mentorship, guidance and expertise to small businesses. The funding will allow SBDCs, WBCs, and MBDCs to hire staff and provide programming to help small businesses and minority-owned businesses respond to COVID-19. The bill also provides funds for the associations that represent SBDCs and WBCs to create a joint platform that consolidates information and resources related to COVID-19 in order to provide consistent, timely information to small businesses. The SCORE mentoring program and Veterans Business Outreach Center program are encouraged to use the platform and participate in the COVID-19 education sessions for their volunteer mentors and small business counselors. (From "Cardin, Bipartisan Senate Task Force Secure $377 Billion for Small Business," US Senate Committee on Small Business & Entrepreneurship, press release.)

23 "Evaluating the Costs of Government Credit Support During the COVID-19," Hong and Lucas

24 "The Job Preservation Effects of Paycheck Protection Program Loans," Faulkender, Jackman, and Miran

Protection Program and Health Care Enhancement Act, with funding starting by April 27.[25] A third tranche of approximately $285 billion was authorized for distribution in late December 2020 as part of the Economic Aid to Hard-Hit Small Businesses, Nonprofits, and Venues Act—which also permitted a "second draw" by eligible small businesses that could demonstrate an impact to their revenue due to circumstances associated with the COVID-19 pandemic.[26]

Notwithstanding its criticisms, the PPP's design resulted in approximately 95 percent of loans being forgiven by the SBA, an organization which had only guaranteed $30 billion in traditional small business loans the previous year.[27] The common refrain shared across the SBA community was that the agency had "*processed more than 14 years' worth of loans in less than 14 days*."[28] And the numbers were staggering, with thousands of

25 "The Job Preservation Effects of Paycheck Protection Program Loans," Faulkender, Jackman, and Miran

26 "The Job Preservation Effects of Paycheck Protection Program Loans," Faulkender, Jackman, and Miran

27 "Evaluating the Role of the Paycheck Protection Program During COVID-19," panel discussion between R. Glenn Hubbard, Dean Emeritus, and Russell L. Carson, Professor of Finance and Economics, Columbia University; and David Autor, Ford Professor, and Margaret MacVicar, Faculty Fellow, MIT Department of Economics, moderated by M-RCBG Senior Fellow Aparna Mathur, January 20, 2023, https://www.hks.harvard.edu/events/evaluating-role-paycheck-protection-program-during-COVID-19; "A Discussion of Small Business and Worker Support Programs During the Pandemic," panel discussion between David Autor, Ford Professor of Economics, MIT; Jacob Mortenson, economist, Joint Committee on Taxation; Giulia Giupponi, Assistant Professor of Public Economics, Bocconi University; and Ruth Simon, senior special writer, *Wall Street Journal*; moderated by former M-RCBG Senior Fellow Aparna Mathur, February 15, 2024, https://www.hks.harvard.edu/events/discussion-small-business-and-worker-support-programs-during-pandemic

28 "As Small Business Loan Money Runs Out, Many Approved Businesses Still Await Checks or Clarity on Strict Guidelines," Tom Huddleston Jr., CNBC, April 17, 2020, https://www.cnbc.com/2020/04/17/small-businesses-await-checks-clarity-as-ppp-loan-program-runs-dry.html

lenders making 1.7 million loans at an average amount of just over $200,000 between April 3 and April 16, 2020.[29] Alongside this effort, the Federal Reserve provided certain liquidity facilities to support these programs—namely the Paycheck Protection Program Liquidity Facility (PPPLF) to help sustain lender capabilities, as well as its associated Main Street Lending Program—to purchase participation in loans to small and mid-sized businesses by eligible lenders.[30]

Alongside appropriations for SBA's disaster loan program, a separate and distinct $10 billion grant program was also passed in the CARES Act and championed by Senator Ben Cardin of Maryland as part of the Emergency Injury Disaster Loan (EIDL) product suite.[31] This EIDL program was built on the back of the existing SBA direct disaster lending capability, which is essentially a very low-interest loan available to borrowers impacted by federally declared disasters, most often seen in single state or regional circumstances, such as hurricanes and wildfires. However, the novel product in this instance was truly unprecedented in that it offered small businesses forgivable grants of $1,000 per employee, up to a maximum of $10,000 per business applicant.[32] While the

29 "The $800 Billion Paycheck Protection Program," Autor et al.

30 "Paycheck Protection Program Liquidity Facility," Board of Governors of the Federal Reserve System, https://www.federalreserve.gov/monetarypolicy/PPPlf.htm; "Main Street Lending Program," Board of Governors of the Federal Reserve System, https://www.federalreserve.gov/monetarypolicy/mainstreetlending.htm#:~:text=The%20Federal%20Reserve%20established%20the,terminated%20on%20January%208%2C%202021

31 "Senator Ben Cardin Response to COVID-19," Global Chamber, March 27, 2020, https://www.globalchamber.org/blog/2020/03/27/global-chamber/senator-ben-cardin-response-to-covid-19/?lpct=ODguYS4yMDIwLTEwLTA4

32 *Emergency Economic Injury Grants: The stimulus includes $10 billion in funding for a provision to provide an advance of $10,000 to small businesses and nonprofits that apply for an SBA economic injury disaster loan (EIDL) within three days of applying for the loan. EIDLs are loans of up to $2 million that carry interest rates*

grant component of this program was understandably incredibly popular, evidenced by the fact that it ran out of money in just fourteen weeks, it experienced significant technology and administrative disruptions and outright closures. As access to every dollar possible was so crucial in the early days of the COVID-19 pandemic, the challenges associated with both this grant program and traditional disaster lending took center stage.[33]

In fact, in a House Small Business Committee hearing on July 1, 2020, with respect to the administration of these EIDL grants and the overall performance of the agency, then Chair Nydia Velázquez, a Democrat from New York, opened the hearing with critical words, stating, "*Even more troubling is the fact that the SBA has not communicated well with applicants, nor has it provided them with reliable ways to check the status of their applications. Borrowers are simply told that the loan is processing. The only*

---

up to 3.75 percent for companies and up to 2.75 percent for nonprofits, as well as principal and interest deferment for up to 4 years. The loans may be used to pay for expenses that could have been met had the disaster not occurred, including payroll and other operating expenses. The EIDL grant does not need to be repaid, even if the grantee is subsequently denied an EIDL, and may be used to provide paid sick leave to employees, maintaining payroll, meet increased production costs due to supply chain disruptions, or pay business obligations, including debts, rent and mortgage payments. Eligible grant recipients must have been in operation on January 31, 2020. The grant is available to small businesses, private nonprofits, sole proprietors and independent contractors, tribal businesses, as well as cooperatives and employee-owned businesses. A business that receives an EIDL between January 31, 2020, and June 30, 2020 as a result of a COVID-19 disaster declaration is eligible to apply for a PPP loan or the business may refinance their EIDL into a PPP loan. In either case, the emergency EIDL grant award of up to $10,000 would be subtracted from the amount forgiven in the Paycheck Protection Plan. The bill provides $562 million to ensure that SBA has the resources to provide Economic Injury Disaster Loans (EIDL) to businesses that need financial support." (From "Cardin, Bipartisan Senate Task Force Secure $377 Billion for Small Businesses," US Senate Committee on Small Business and Entrepreneurship, press release.)

33 "SBA Grant Program Attracting Wrong Kind of Attention," David Lynch, *Washington Post*, July 15, 2020, https://www.washingtonpost.com/business/2020/07/15/sba-eidl-loan-program-coronavirus/

other updates they receive are whether the loan has been approved or denied. Applicants need to know where they stand in the queue so they know how much longer they must wait before receiving financing. And given the current economic climate, if they are going to be denied, they deserve to know quickly so that they can explore options for capital elsewhere. Finally, there was a long period during which the EIDL application portal was limited to only agricultural small businesses, which is completely at odds with the intent of the Small Business Act and the mission of the SBA, which is to aid, counsel, assist, and protect the interests of all small businesses."[34] Her Republican colleague Steve Chabot, ranking member of the committee, expressed similar concerns when he conveyed that "*[w]hile EIDL loans are being processed and the Advance grants are being disbursed, too many small businesses are left with questions—questions on communication, questions on the status of their loan, and questions surrounding the maximum loan amount under the program.*"[35] The EIDL program would later be shown as a frequent target for illicit activity by the SBA's Office of the Inspector General, which identified that insufficient risk mitigations were put into place at its inception, potentially resulting in billions of dollars of fraud.[36]

Finally, in March 2021, President Joe Biden signed the American Rescue Plan, which notably extended certain unemployment benefits, advanced further direct stimulus payments to

34 "The Economic Injury Disaster Loan Program: Status Update from the Administration," hearing before the US House Committee on Small Business, US Government Publishing Office, July 1, 2020, https://www.govinfo.gov/content/pkg/CHRG-116hhrg41295/html/CHRG-116hhrg41295.htm

35 "The Economic Injury Disaster Loan Program," hearing before the US House Committee on Small Business

36 "SBA Overpaid $4.5 Billion on 'Illogical' Small Business Grant Claims," Stacy Cowley, *New York Times*, October 7, 2021, https://www.nytimes.com/2021/10/07/business/fraud-small-business-administration.html

the American public, authorized additional funding for PPP and EIDL grants, extended eligibility to other nonprofits, and established a targeted industry support program (e.g., the Restaurant Revitalization Fund and the Shuttered Venue Operators Grant).[37] The SBA ceased taking PPP applications on May 31, 2021, having guaranteed almost twelve million loans through nearly 5,500 lenders for a total of approximately $800 billion, with an average loan size of $67,647.[38] By March 6, 2022, approximately 85 percent of those loans, just over $700 billion, had been forgiven.[39]

So, it is clear that based on size alone, the main event at the SBA to support the small business community was the PPP, and for that to work, unlike the EIDL program, much of that heavy lifting was on the capabilities, systems, and human resources of national and community-based financial lenders to get these resources into the hands of the American people. It is estimated that banks made 93 percent of the loans associated with the first tranche of PPP funding, and the evidence ultimately demonstrates that the PPP lending was overall commensurate with population demographics.[40]

---

37 "American Rescue Plan," The White House, https://www.whitehouse.gov/american-rescue-plan/#:~:text=The%20American%20Rescue%20Plan%20provides%20a%20100%25%20federal%20continuation%20health,t%20lose%20their%20health%20care

38 "An Empirical Review of the Paycheck Protection Program," hearing before US House Committee on Small Business Subcommittee on Oversight, Investigations and Regulations, March 16, 2022, https://docs.house.gov/Committee/Calendar/ByEvent.aspx?EventID=114490

39 "An Empirical Review of the Paycheck Protection Program," hearing before US House Committee on Small Business Subcommittee on Oversight, Investigations and Regulations"

40 "An Empirical Review of the Paycheck Protection Program," hearing before US House Committee on Small Business Subcommittee on Oversight, Investigations and Regulations; *Paycheck Protection Program: Program Changes Increased Lending to the Smallest Businesses and in Underserved Locations*, US Government Accountability Office report to Congress, September 2021, https://www.gao.gov/products/gao-21-601

This was almost certainly due in part to the role of many community banks, credit unions, minority depository institutions (MDIs), and community development financial institutions, the latter of which were able to access a $10 billion set-aside amount in May 2020, and alongside MDIs, were provided an exclusive window for PPP lending on January 11, 2021.[41] Given the options at the time, while it is hard to envision a program that would have gotten money into the hands of American workers much faster than the PPP model, ensuring that lenders engaged with underserved communities are well-positioned early on in any pandemic lending program is important. Over the course of the PPP lending, loans to women-owned businesses doubled from the first phase to the second, up to 18 percent; lending to veteran-owned businesses was pretty consistent throughout the program at about 5 percent; and capital to businesses with fewer than ten employees jumped from 9 percent in the first phase to 86 percent by the third tranche of funding.[42] With respect to these smallest of businesses, part of the rationale for a delay in early access may have been attributable to their ability to apply for and receive funding from other early pandemic programs, such as the Pandemic Unemployment Insurance program or the EIDL grants.[43]

In all, the sheer number of lenders, amount of funding made available, and the size and speed of the program was unlike almost any other financial response that the United States had

41 *Paycheck Protection Program: Program Changes Increased Lending to the Smallest Businesses,* US Government Accountability Office report

42 *Paycheck Protection Program: Program Changes Increased Lending to the Smallest Businesses,* US Government Accountability Office report

43 *Paycheck Protection Program: Program Changes Increased Lending to the Smallest Businesses,* US Government Accountability Office report

ever undertaken. And while many of the key policy crafters from the Treasury, SBA, and White House were in the office every day, many government and private sector employees were doing their part to implement this novel program, mostly working from home, educating their children from home, and facing the same health fears and challenges that so many Americans were facing during this time. Input and ideas came from every imaginable outlet—past policymakers, university professors, and the media, for example—but there were no textbooks to study and only limited real-time research to advance the economic remedy sought. In fact, as Columbia economics professor and former Columbia Business School Dean Glenn Hubbard recalled, he engaged with the Senate in advance of the program, and he shared that the only real way to get that kind of money out the door was through the banks that already had these relationships in place.[44] A true public-private partnership.

Insights from experts will be imperative for the economic response to the next pandemic, and all of those who are willing to share their constructive criticisms and proactive solutions should be consulted and encouraged to document information that will be useful to the next generation of decision-makers. In fact, Dr. Osler did just that for his students. When he lived in Baltimore at One West Franklin Street, he was well known for establishing one of the great private medical libraries in his home. In line with his well-known commitment to his students, he offered keys to his home and library to certain favored medical residents and pupils so that they could utilize the books within his library—day or

44 "Evaluating the Role of the Paycheck Protection Program During COVID-19," panel discussion; "A Discussion of Small Business and Worker Support Programs During the Pandemic," panel discussion

night. These individuals would be known as the "latchkeyers" for how often they would freely enter the Osler residence to review his various treatises.[45] This practice continued in his London residence while at Oxford University, which included vast gatherings of medical professionals throughout the halls of his home.[46]

In fact, on any given night, one could find an impromptu assembly of dozens of students or practicing physicians in his salon discussing contemporary medical topics and sharing ideas and techniques that could potentially lead to health care breakthroughs. As the former head of the British Medical Association and Royal Society of Medicine wrote, "*As Osler so clearly indicated many years ago, clinical and laboratory science, combined with communication skills, must continue to be partners in our aim of serving as best we can our patients, future patients, knowledge itself and society. These may be truisms but it is upon their full recognition and application in our everyday contact with patients and in the Osler tradition that good clinical practice depends.*"[47]

45 *Sir William Osler: An Encyclopedia*, Charles S. Bryan, ed., (Norman Publishing, 2020)

46 "Sir William Osler, Oxford, and 'The Open Arms,'" Lord Walton of Detchant, *West of England Medical Journal*, vol. 7, no. 2, August 1992; available at NIH National Library of Medicine, https://www.ncbi.nlm.nih.gov/

47 "Sir William Osler, Oxford and 'The Open Arms,'" Walton

SECTION II

The Benefits & The Complications

CHAPTER THREE

Successful Impacts of the PPP on Small Businesses

The good physician treats the disease; the great physician treats the patient who has the disease.

IN THEIR WRITING *OSLER FOR White Coat Pockets,* all-things-Osler expert Dr. Charles Bryan and his colleague Dr. Joseph VanderVeer Jr. discussed Dr. Osler's focus on humanizing the patient. Based on his tutelage, their approach to clinical teaching was to encourage students to realize that the "*task is to make this patient seem like the most interesting human being in this country—a person that everyone should feel privileged to help!*" Citing multiple examples of personal diagnostic success based on a keen and curious interest, the pair even conveyed the idea in an economic sense, sharing that "*obtaining a meaningful social history need not take a lot of time and pays huge dividends down the road.*"[1] One of the more memorable anecdotes provided is about a very well-known California physician, Dr. Faith Fitzgerald at

1 *Osler for White Coat Pockets: A Vade Mecum for Medical Students and Residents,* Joseph B. VanderVeer, MD, and Charles Bryan, MD, American Osler Society (Masthof Press, 2017)

San Francisco General Hospital. Dr. Fitzgerald was determined to teach her students that "*there are no uninteresting patients, just uninterested doctors.*"[2] At her suggestion, while visiting patients, she asked a resident to pick the patient who was believed to be the least interesting patient on the hospital floor. The resident picked a very quiet elderly woman who had recently been evicted from her apartment. And so, Dr. Fitzgerald began her examination:

Doctor: "Have you ever been to a hospital before?"

Patient: "Once."

Doctor: "What for?"

Patient: "I broke my arm."

Doctor: "How did you break your arm?"

Patient: "A trunk fell on it."

Doctor: "What kind of trunk?"

Patient: "A steamer trunk."

Doctor: "How did that happen?"

Patient: "The boat lurched."

Doctor: "Why did the boat lurch?"

Patient: "It hit an iceberg."

Patient: "What was the name of the boat?"

Doctor: "The Titanic."[3]

The unique life tale of this woman as a genuine survivor of one of the most well-known decades-old tragedies went on

2 *Osler for White Coat Pockets*, VanderVeer and Bryan
3 *Osler for White Coat Pockets*, VanderVeer and Bryan

to become so noteworthy that it was captured by newspapers and television—making her instantly one of the most famous people in San Francisco and dramatically changing her life circumstances.[4] This is a perfect example of understanding the individual story of a patient and the impact that their personal traumas may have had on their diagnosis and treatment. Drs. Bryan and VanderVeer went on to reiterate Dr. Osler's warning that there is a tendency for young doctors "*to study the cases, not the patients, and in the interest they take in the disease, lose sight of the individual*."[5] In short, while the disease must be identified and treated accordingly, there are unique characteristics to particular patients, and those two narratives of malady and circumstances are inseparable. Their past health, their family history, and their individual social and economic circumstances may in fact hold the key to a regimen of treatment and lifestyle changes that could result in the mutual goal of healing.

As has been demonstrated, the economic challenge of the COVID-19 pandemic was widespread, and not unlike the prescribed bedside manner of the good doctor, the PPP was designed with small businesses and their employees as the proverbial patients. While the economy at large is the macro-beneficiary of such a federal stimulus program, the ultimate success of this kind of initiative is only achieved by one employer and one employee at a time. With that in mind, the federal government had the difficult job of balancing an expedited legislative initiative with the development of an immediate operational model that could effectively distribute funding in an almost real-time manner, so as to make the program both viable and impactful.

4 *Osler for White Coat Pockets*, VanderVeer and Bryan

5 *Osler for White Coat Pockets*, VanderVeer and Bryan

And by many accounts, much of this was achieved. With more than eleven million loans ultimately processed, in accordance with Professor Hubbard's advice to the Senate, there is certainly a case to be made that the unique distribution model was the best option available under the circumstances.

In fact, a common refrain among many small businesses that sincerely benefited from the intent of the legislation is that while the program may be criticized for how it worked, *it worked for them.* It kept family businesses open, preserved the opportunity for longtime employees to stay connected to their employers, and allowed those employees to maintain health insurance—which was, of course, critical during such a public health emergency. But notwithstanding the anecdotal evidence, the PPP undoubtedly demonstrated significant challenges that must be accounted for in any future events. And just like any medical assessment, the physician/policymaker must learn the history of the processes, procedures, and treatments that worked for the patient, hear from them directly about the components that might have been designed better, and ensure that those lessons are duplicated and incorporated into any potential future diagnoses and treatments as appropriate. In that light, this chapter will seek to show where the program design of PPP succeeded in putting the small business patient first.[6]

Given its intention, the most important success of the PPP was that it saved jobs. The reason this was the most critical component is that it was, in fact, the clearly stated policy goal. In

6 "The $800 Billion Paycheck Protection Program: Where Did the Money Go and Why Did It Go There?" David Autor, David Cho, Leland D. Crane, Mita Goldar, Byron Lutz, Joshua Montes, William B. Peterman, David Ratner, Daniel Villar, and Ahu Yildirmaz, National Bureau of Economic Research, January 2022, https://www.nber.org/system/files/working_papers/w29669/w29669.pdf

many ways it was not meant to serve as a traditional stimulus program per se, but rather to ensure the continuity of the employed workforce.[7] As discussed by Professor Hubbard, the particular concern of Republican congressional leadership at the time of the CARES Act debate was that extended shutdowns could substantially impact aggregate demand, thus creating something of an economic "*doom loop*."[8] And beyond just saving jobs, according to Hubbard, the evidence surrounding the PPP suggested that it not only "*substantially increased the employment, financial health, and survival of small businesses*," but also "*was most effective for relatively smaller firms*."[9]

Now, of course the question is how many jobs did it actually save? Senator Rubio, one of the key architects of the plan, assessed early on that "*[a]cross the United States, the PPP helped support up to 55 million jobs, including up to 4.5 million in manufacturing, with an average firm size of just 20 employees*," not-

7 "Evaluating the Role of the Paycheck Protection Program During COVID-19," panel discussion between R. Glenn Hubbard, Dean Emeritus, and Russell L. Carson, Professor of Finance and Economics, Columbia University; and David Autor, Ford Professor, and Margaret MacVicar, Faculty Fellow, MIT Department of Economics; moderated by M-RCBG Senior Fellow Aparna Mathur, January 20, 2023, https://www.hks.harvard.edu/events/evaluating-role-paycheck-protection-program-during-COVID-19; "A Discussion of Small Business and Worker Support Programs During the Pandemic," panel discussion between David Autor, Ford Professor of Economics, MIT; Jacob Mortenson, economist, Joint Committee on Taxation; Giulia Giupponi, Assistant Professor of Public Economics, Bocconi University; and Ruth Simon, senior special writer, *Wall Street Journal*; moderated by former M-RCBG Senior Fellow Aparna Mathur, February 15, 2024, https://www.hks.harvard.edu/events/discussion-small-business-and-worker-support-programs-during-pandemic

8 "Evaluating the Role of the Paycheck Protection Program During COVID-19," panel discussion; "A Discussion of Small Business and Worker Support Programs During the Pandemic," panel discussion

9 "Has the Paycheck Protection Program Succeeded?" Glenn Hubbard and Michael R. Strain, IZA Institute of Labor Economics, IZA Discussion Paper No. 13808, October 2020, https://docs.iza.org/dp13808.pdf

ing that while the final numbers may vary, the evidence would support a figure in this magnitude.[10] Financial services giants, such as JPMorgan Chase's CEO Jamie Dimon, have estimated the number of jobs saved to be as high as somewhere between thirty and thirty-five million, whereas some groups, like Standard & Poor's, have estimated this number to be closer to 13.6 million.[11] Yet others, like Goldman Sachs' Chief Economist David Mericle, have taken more of a qualitive approach that characterized the PPP's success in light of what "*had the potential to be a huge collapse*."[12] Regardless of where one falls on this possible spectrum, this quantitative range of double-digit millions of jobs continues to be the subject of debate by academics and economists, as some have argued that the success of the program was only a fraction of these estimates—closer to saving, for example, more in the neighborhood of three million positions.[13]

This is, of course, a pretty massive range, but even those whose research supports the lower end of the job spectrum share the idea that, given the circumstances, the PPP was the right course of action at the time.[14] One rationale for this differential is

---

10 "Rubio Details Historic Success of the Paycheck Protection Program," US Senator Marco Rubio, press release, December 10, 2020, https://www.rubio.senate.gov/rubio-details-historic-success-of-the-paycheck-protection-program/

11 "The Job Preservation Effects of Paycheck Protection Program Loans," Michael Faulkender, Robert Jackman, and Stephen Miran, *Social Science Research*, February 15, 2023; available at SSRN: https://ssrn.com/abstract=3767509 or http://dx.doi.org/10.2139/ssrn.3767509

12 "The Job Preservation Effects of Paycheck Protection Program Loans," Faulkender, Jackman, and Miran

13 "The Job Preservation Effects of Paycheck Protection Program Loans," Faulkender, Jackman, and Miran

14 "Evaluating the Role of the Paycheck Protection Program During COVID-19," panel discussion; "A Discussion of Small Business and Worker Support Programs During the Pandemic," panel discussion

the data sets used by the reviewers. Under standard SBA policy, a small business in America is limited to those entities that employ fewer than five hundred people; however, some research shows that as much as 85 percent of the first $525 billion of PPP dollars was utilized by firms with fewer than one hundred employees.[15] It stands to reason that these smaller firms were more impacted by the circumstances of the COVID-19 virus, particularly those that employed just a handful of people. As the sample set of PPP recipients grows to larger firms, that population was more likely to have access to financial reserves, lines of credit, and fixed customer contracts, all of which tend to make them more resilient in such circumstances.[16] And even if smaller firms had access to capital for normal business operations, particularly under these conditions, bank credit would likely have dragged on for months if obtainable at all, which would provide cold comfort to those that would not be able to survive the COVID-19 pandemic without some sort of PPP-style funding.[17]

Based on results from a US Census Bureau Small Business Pulse Survey from May 2020, it can be extrapolated that the majority of PPP recipients would not have had enough cash on hand to sustain their employee base through the COVID-19 pandemic.[18] This became even more impactful on the smallest of businesses whose ability to withstand the conditions could have

15 "The Job Preservation Effects of Paycheck Protection Program Loans," Faulkender, Jackman, and Miran

16 "The Job Preservation Effects of Paycheck Protection Program Loans," Faulkender, Jackman, and Miran

17 "The Job Preservation Effects of Paycheck Protection Program Loans," Faulkender, Jackman, and Miran

18 "The Job Preservation Effects of Paycheck Protection Program Loans," Faulkender, Jackman, and Miran

been limited to just a few weeks.[19] In a more conventional economic environment, this would have led to massive business closures and bankruptcies; however, the evidence demonstrates that even in this extreme situation, there was only a modest increase in bankruptcies during this time.[20] In fact, the US Council of Economic Advisers, a White House organization that assembles and analyzes economic data for the president's policymaking consideration, showed that while bankruptcies increased in February and March 2020, for the period of April through June of that same year, levels of business bankruptcies were lower than expected, even as forecasted before the first case of the COVID-19 virus was even diagnosed.[21]

University of Maryland Smith Business School Professor and former Assistant Treasury Secretary for Economic Policy Michael Faulkender uses just this argument to show that the ability of so many smaller firms to avoid closure illustrates the strength of the PPP as a robust policy response and provides a sound economic argument that the PPP may have saved as many as twenty-five million jobs.[22] According to Professor Faulkender and his team, early PPP loans gained significant saturation in the marketplace—particularly with smaller businesses, at an average cost of between $34,300 and $37,000 per job.[23] Their research went on

19 "The Job Preservation Effects of Paycheck Protection Program Loans," Faulkender, Jackman, and Miran

20 "The Job Preservation Effects of Paycheck Protection Program Loans," Faulkender, Jackman, and Miran

21 "The Job Preservation Effects of Paycheck Protection Program Loans," Faulkender, Jackman, and Miran

22 "The Job Preservation Effects of Paycheck Protection Program Loans," Faulkender, Jackman, and Miran

23 "The Job Preservation Effects of Paycheck Protection Program Loans," Faulkender, Jackman, and Miran

to point out that in March 2020, surveys also demonstrated that small business owners' expectations were that they would have had to cut workforce by up to 40 percent, but after becoming aware of the PPP, that number fell to just 6 percent—which, upon extrapolation of the nearly sixty million small business that took PPP loans, implies support of at least twenty million jobs.[24]

While in agreement that the PPP was still likely the best option available to policymakers, Professor David Autor of the Massachusetts Institute of Technology assessed the results of the program somewhat differently.[25] Whereas Professor Autor and his colleagues acknowledge that the PPP ensured that smaller businesses did receive vital funds, his position is that the PPP lacked efficiency in that it "*was essentially untargeted, aside from excluding firms with more than 500 workers.*"[26] Professor Autor and his colleagues argue that the PPP may have preserved somewhere around three million jobs, at an average of approximately $170,000 to $285,000 per job, a figure that was significantly above the average salary metrics for the jobs in scope.[27] As such, they submit that this program inefficiency led to many businesses accessing PPP that did not truly need the funding, costing the American taxpayers more than it should have.[28] While noting the soundness of the design employed here, Professor Faulkender and his colleagues account for the differences in their assessment

24 "The Job Preservation Effects of Paycheck Protection Program Loans," Faulkender, Jackman, and Miran

25 "The $800 Billion Paycheck Protection Program," Autor et al.

26 "The $800 Billion Paycheck Protection Program," Autor et al.

27 "The $800 Billion Paycheck Protection Program," Autor et al.

28 "Evaluating the Role of the Paycheck Protection Program During COVID-19," panel discussion; "A Discussion of Small Business and Worker Support Programs During the Pandemic," panel discussion

as being due to the fact that they concentrated on a smaller firm population.[29]

An interesting point made by Professor Autor and his colleagues is that the third tranche of PPP funding did not have an appreciable impact on the employment numbers, perhaps due to some level of economic improvement by that time.[30] If that is the case, it may make sense to examine any future pandemic in two parts: an initial "Rescue Period" and a subsequent "Recovery Period," where, in fact, various other small businesses and worker support models could be investigated beyond the initial large-scale stimulus actions. This framework was actually utilized in other countries with loans and other debt vehicles in the early days of the COVID-19 pandemic and then ultimately something of a pivot to other financial and technical assistance approaches a few months later.[31] But for these purposes, to the point of the effect of the PPP, there is nearly unanimous agreement that while the program may not have been perfect, it can still be viewed as the right thing to have done given the circumstances.[32] And with an approximately 95 percent take-up rate by the eligible small

29 "The Job Preservation Effects of Paycheck Protection Program Loans," Faulkender, Jackman, and Miran

30 "The $800 Billion Paycheck Protection Program," Autor et al.

31 *Financing SMEs and Entrepreneurs 2022: SME Finance in COVID-19 Recovery Packages: Assessment and Implications*, Organisation for Economic Co-Operation and Development report (Paris: OECD Publishing, 2022), https://www.oecd-ilibrary.org/sites/44db9703-en/index.html?itemId=/content/component/44db9703-en

32 *"These outcomes should not however be viewed first and foremost as programmatic failures. Given the time constraints and, more profoundly, the lack of existing administrative infrastructure for overseeing targeted federal support to the entire population of US small businesses at the onset of the pandemic, we strongly suspect that Congress could not have better targeted the PPP without substantially slowing its delivery."* (From "The $800 Billion Paycheck Protection Program," Autor et al.)

business community and a comparable partial/full forgiveness percentage, regardless of where you ultimately stand on the number of workers the program protected, the fact that the PPP saved jobs is not in dispute.[33]

And while politics was an ever-present backdrop to the COVID-19 pandemic, another notable success of the PPP was the ability for elected officials to meet the moment in a bipartisan manner. While Congress and the White House quite rightfully engaged in genuine political discourse—in and out of the partisan spotlight—they embraced the core components of what policymaking is all about. In contemporary society, this type of success has been unique, but of course so were the circumstances and timeline associated with the COVID-19 pandemic. There was not 100 percent agreement on everything, and it did not happen overnight, but it did happen in near-record time. And while political barbs were exchanged across the aisle both privately and publicly, rational men and women came together to achieve what history will see as a pivotal moment of the twenty-first century.

In hindsight, though, people may mistakenly take this colossal mission for granted. Imagine just what that took: Getting Republicans and Democrats in the House of Representatives to be on board. Getting Democrats and Republicans in the Senate to be aligned. Ensuring that there was the political will throughout the entire executive branch of government—including offices such as the Office of Management and Budget and the Department of the Treasury and, of course, the President of the United States. And

33 "Evaluating the Role of the Paycheck Protection Program During COVID-19," panel discussion; "A Discussion of Small Business and Worker Support Programs During the Pandemic," panel discussion

even then, after the herculean task of achieving sufficient legislative harmony among all these individuals, there was the effort to ensure that the private sector distribution models of the banks, credit unions, minority depository institutions, farm credit lenders, community development financial institutions, and ultimately the fintech firms, among others, were able to support the goals and activities associated with this model.

In all congressional negotiations, members must make numerous decisions on policy goals, size of appropriations, allocation of responsibilities across federal agencies, and gauge the support in Congress and by the public at large for a particular legislative approach. By constitutional design, this process is intended to last months or even years and is completed on an expedited basis only in exceptional circumstances. However, by the second week in March 2020, the severity of the COVID-19 pandemic was becoming clear, and the economic realities became very apparent in an accelerated fashion.

Policy advice and ideas were shared with the White House and Congress both privately and publicly. One such public advisory came from Harvard Kennedy School professor and former chair of the Council of Economic Advisers in the Obama administration Jason Furman, who penned an opinion piece in the *Wall Street Journal* on March 5. He wrote that on top of the medical needs associated with the COVID-19 virus, "*Congress should act swiftly but thoughtfully to pass fiscal stimulus*" in an amount as high as $350 billion, and higher if necessary.[34] Given Professor Furman's experience during the Great Recession, his recommen-

34 "The Case for a Big Coronavirus Stimulus," Jason Furman, *Wall Street Journal*, March 5, 2020, https://www.wsj.com/articles/the-case-for-a-big-coronavirus-stimulus-11583448500

dations were a thoughtful assessment of the circumstances, but everyone knew any proposed solution could prove challenging under the accelerated timelines before the country.

In the same vein, just like the private sector industrialization for the nation's wartime priorities or the research and development initiatives that have led to space travel and significant medical cures, the medical and economic achievements of this period should be well-placed in the category of greatest public-private partnerships of all time. Senator Rubio's spokesperson simply assessed the PPP by concluding that "*[a]t the end of the day, if there's a way to keep people connected to employment, that's what we wanted to do.*"[35] And that really was accomplished. But it wasn't done in a vacuum. For all its criticisms, there were government employees, lending professionals, and small businesses that mobilized to support a large chunk of the economy and its workforce. As summed up by JPMorgan Chase CEO Dimon, "*Thousands of dedicated (staff) worked tirelessly...to support the federal government in one of the largest and most ambitious emergency lending facilities in history.*"[36] There would be plenty to disagree about over the course of the COVID-19 pandemic: the size of subsequent legislation, the timing of lockdowns, the use of funds by state leaders. But for that day in March, both sides came together for the American people.

But as has been noted, the PPP was not the only initiative on the table to support American workers. Stimulus checks and

---

35 "Small-Business Owners Say PPP Isn't the Solution They Need," Devin Leonard, Bloomberg, May 7, 2020, https://www.bloomberg.com/news/features/2020-05-07/small-business-owners-say-ppp-isn-t-covid-19-solution-they-need

36 "JPMorgan Chase Approved to Process $15 Billion in New PPP Loans," Elizabeth Dilts Marshall, Reuters, May 1, 2020, https://www.reuters.com/article/idUSKBN22D5X1/ (parentheses in original)

unemployment insurance appropriations were also made available by Congress. That said, while some critics have argued that the country should have relied entirely on the use of unemployment insurance, as opposed to the additional development of the PPP, the evidence demonstrates that the use of both programs contemporaneously was a policy success.[37] Like any good physician might do when entering the patient's room, he or she must examine the patient's chart, which outlines the diagnosis of the illness and the actions taken to date. And this chart of the American economy in those early days of COVID-19 showed the loss of millions of jobs cascading into historic unemployment—at a rate nearly ten times worse than the financial crisis of the Great Recession.[38]

With business closures mounting, ongoing layoffs, and an imposing economic contraction estimate for the second quarter of 2020, one solution could have been the development of an enormous unemployment backstop designed to protect workers and the larger economy from an immense labor disruption. While this was of course on the list of possible policy approaches to these circumstances at the beginning of this process—and was certainly one of the tools that was ultimately utilized through a companion program called Pandemic Unemployment Assistance (PUA)—the sheer size of these layoffs coupled with an antiquated state unemployment payment infrastructure was simply not tenable as the single measure to support small businesses and their employees during this period.[39]

37 "Evaluating the Role of the Paycheck Protection Program During COVID-19," panel discussion; "A Discussion of Small Business and Worker Support Programs During the Pandemic," panel discussion

38 "The Job Preservation Effects of Paycheck Protection Program Loans," Faulkender, Jackman, and Miran

39 "The Job Preservation Effects of Paycheck Protection Program Loans," Faulkender, Jackman, and Miran

With a key rationale for the PPP being that keeping the employee connected to the business would also benefit the business owner since they would not have the administrative burden of rehiring personnel once the crisis had passed, the combination of PPP and unemployment insurance did demonstrate a rather fascinating policy strategy. Did the PPP really keep workers tied to firms? Even if employees were let go, could they have been hired elsewhere? Certainly, a general position that supports efficient labor market reallocation seems sensible. But, of course, the unique nature of these circumstances reasonably required some kind of intervention to bridge between this uncertain time and the period of stability that would ultimately follow—unfortunately, no one knew when that would be.[40] That said, the role of unemployment insurance is an important question and one that is worth exploring in the context of the PPP.

For purposes of background, federal unemployment insurance has been around since 1935 as a product of the Franklin D. Roosevelt administration and is intended as a temporary program to pay partial wages to those laid off while they seek gainful employment.[41] Although the program is overseen by the US Department of Labor, it is administered by the individual states, which are generally allowed to set their own criteria and benefits in accordance with federal guidelines.[42] Benefits typically last up to twenty-six weeks and can be extended under certain condi-

40 "Evaluating the Role of the Paycheck Protection Program During COVID-19," panel discussion; "A Discussion of Small Business and Worker Support Programs During the Pandemic," panel discussion

41 "Introduction to Unemployment Insurance," Chad Stone and William Chen, Center on Budget and Policy Priorities, March 24, 2020, https://www.cbpp.org/research/introduction-to-unemployment-insurance

42 "Introduction to Unemployment Insurance," Stone and Chen

tions.[43] As part of the legislative response to the Great Recession, the 2009 American Recovery and Reinvestment Act distributed funds to dozens of states to modernize their unemployment programs.[44] While the unemployment system is intended to be forward-funded by an employer tax, many states have adopted a pay-as-you-go approach. As a result, several of these systems have not been well-prepared during periods of economic downturn and have resorted to borrowing funding from the federal government.[45]

Given that the unemployment insurance program is something of a decentralized model that often depends on intermittent support from the federal government, its administration can be rife with challenges. Beyond just the funding issue, these dozens of individual state and territory systems have had no meaningful technology updates in decades. In fact, many of these systems were programmed using the very outdated COBOL computer language, and in March 2020, policymakers knew that their reliability would likely come into question for any unique approach undertaken for the COVID-19 pandemic.[46] Given an inability for true federal oversight of what would be a potential massive block of funds spread among a plethora of antiquated state technologies that would likely contribute to delays, disruptions, and potential fraud, this approach was not selected as the blanket response.[47]

---

43 "Introduction to Unemployment Insurance," Stone and Chen

44 "Introduction to Unemployment Insurance," Stone and Chen

45 "Introduction to Unemployment Insurance," Stone and Chen

46 "Evaluating the Role of the Paycheck Protection Program During COVID-19," panel discussion; "A Discussion of Small Business and Worker Support Programs During the Pandemic," panel discussion

47 "The Initial Household Spending Response to COVID-19: Evidence from Credit Card Transactions," JPMorgan Chase Institute, May 2020, https://www.jpmorganchase.com/institute/all-topics/financial-health-wealth-creation/initial-household-spending-response-to-covid-19

The PUA, the component of the CARES Act that addressed this issue, initially added $600 a week as a federal unemployment insurance supplement for up to thirty-nine weeks, which included access for gig workers and independent contractors who did not necessarily have an avenue to traditional unemployment insurance.[48] In many cases, the combination of the PUA and existing unemployment insurance programs provided perceived windfalls for some workers who were able to make more on unemployment insurance than they had while working in their jobs.[49] Some have proposed that this may have led some business owners to lay people off under the idea that these individuals would actually do better financially.[50] The PUA saw its share of fraud, along with the technology constraints, manual reviews, and payment backlogs, but during those days of the COVID-19 pandemic, improper payment review took a back seat to simply getting the money out the door.[51]

And just like the stresses on the operations of the PPP, a less discussed issue was the substantial human capital strain on the state unemployment insurance systems. In fact, it may have been even more significant across the various state systems—including complications around hiring and training, as well as the public pressure for information from elected officials and the media.[52] These actually led to more than a dozen voluntary and involuntary

---

48 "Pandemic Unemployment Fraud in Context," Matt Weidinger and Amy Simon, American Enterprise Institute, January 2024, https://cosm.aei.org/wp-content/uploads/2024/01/Pandemic-Unemployment-Fraud-in-Context.pdf

49 "The Job Preservation Effects of Paycheck Protection Program Loans," Faulkender, Jackman, and Miran

50 "Evaluating the Role of the Paycheck Protection Program During COVID-19," panel discussion; "A Discussion of Small Business and Worker Support Programs During the Pandemic," panel discussion

51 "Pandemic Unemployment Fraud in Context," Weidinger and Simon

52 "Pandemic Unemployment Fraud in Context," Weidinger and Simon

departures of unemployment insurance state directors—some of whom had received claims of death threats.[53] In light of all of these challenges, experts like former Chief of Staff to the US Department of Labor's Employment and Training Administration Amy Simon and her colleague have written extensively on these issues, recommending not only the much-needed technology upgrades to address the delivery and vulnerability issues of the state unemployment insurance systems but also examining possible federal legislation to incentivize state structures to avoid self-certification, harmonize identification, fraud operations, and overpayment measures, as well as establish certain emergency authorities.[54]

With states controlling much of the lockdown and social distancing restrictions early in the COVID-19 pandemic, if unemployment insurance were the sole response, technology failures and fraud could easily have compromised the entire policy response. The tandem of PPP and unemployment insurance sought to balance out some of these factors, and the impact of the design is borne out in the data that showed that while early unemployment insurance claims were historic, the risks associated with that program were offset by the presence of the PPP. The small businesses in receipt of PPP loans could rehire employees quickly so that any initial unemployment insurance claim could be canceled, which would of course reduce the number of approved claims, and those dollars and administrative resources would remain available to employees of businesses that did not participate in PPP.[55]

As most critics recognize that an ill-equipped, digitally challenged, and decentralized state unemployment system prevented

53 "Pandemic Unemployment Fraud in Context," Weidinger and Simon

54 "Pandemic Unemployment Fraud in Context," Weidinger and Simon

55 "The Job Preservation Effects of Paycheck Protection Program Loans," Faulkender, Jackman, and Miran

its capacity as both a sole distribution model and information gathering source, it is generally believed that both state and federal government policy focus going forward should be on modernizing the state unemployment system technologies so that a robust and harmonized model could be more effectively utilized.[56] Some even propose that a reduced hour model for employees, or short-time work, which had been shown to be viable in several European countries through the Great Recession and the COVID-19 pandemic, should be meaningfully piloted beyond just the number of states that have considered this approach in order to test its feasibility for both pandemic and non-pandemic conditions alike.[57]

So, with these headwinds in mind, there was a need for multiple layers of policy innovation to respond to the economic threat of the COVID-19 virus, and not all of it happened at the federal level. In fact, as with any crisis, there is often some type of inventive thinking to make it through unimaginable circumstances to overcome the challenge. During the COVID-19 pandemic, some of those innovations were the novel policy decisions that have already been discussed; some were technological—like the flurry of work-from-home product patents issued, and some were operational—as evidenced by the public-private partnerships with thousands of PPP lenders.[58]

---

56 "Pandemic Unemployment Fraud in Context," Weidinger and Simon

57 "Evaluating the Role of the Paycheck Protection Program During COVID-19," panel discussion; "A Discussion of Small Business and Worker Support Programs During the Pandemic," panel discussion

58 *"The share of new patent applications that advance WFH technologies more than doubles from January to September of 2020, greatly surpassing its previous peak and following an upward trajectory since the onset of the pandemic."* (From "COVID-19 Shifted Patent Applications Toward Technologies that Support Working from Home," American Economic Association, Nicholas Bloom, Steve J. Davis, and Yulia Zhestkova, May 2021, https://www.aeaweb.org/articles?id=10.1257/pandp.20211057.)

That's correct—thousands of PPP lenders. A total of over five thousand lenders, in fact.[59] Even with the operational criticisms, not only did the large banks establish and implement programs—basically overnight—as regulatory guidance was continually updated by officials seeking to ensure program clarity and increase access, but also many other critical lenders stepped in to meet the need to distribute these PPP funds in a timely manner. As mentioned, initially some questioned if SBA was even the right point of delivery for this program. The general position was that SBA was expert at its time-tested loan programs, including its flagship 7(a) small business loan. One private sector veteran of these programs likened the typical SBA experience to that of a pleasant armchair that is comfortable and predictable, and the need for any tweaks is minimal at any given time.

But the question remained as to whether this relatively small agency could now deliver on this brand-new model. In fact, upon the recognition that the SBA would be at the heart of the PPP, some members of the financial services industry opined that it wasn't even really a program that fit neatly within the agency, as the PPP was ultimately more akin to a grant program. Critics suggested that there may be more experienced government organizations to support a program of its makeup, such as the Economic Development Administration within the US Department of Commerce, which, while not front-facing with lenders like the SBA, typically oversees the distribution of billions of dollars in grants. Fortunately, the SBA had the support and expertise of the

59 "PPP Loan Forgiveness: How Do the Top Lenders Compare?" Pandemic Oversight, March 24, 2022, https://www.pandemicoversight.gov/news/articles/PPP-loan-forgiveness-how-do-top-lenders-compare#:~:text=The%20Small%20Business%20Administration%20(SBA,Program%20loans%20through%205%2C000%20lenders

Treasury Department, which had not only served as the chief negotiating agency for the CARES Act, but was positioned to draft rules, engage with lenders, and act affirmatively to tweak the program as permitted by Congress.

Although there was clear recognition by everyone that actions needed to be taken quickly to support small businesses and their employees, some industry leaders struggled to understand the panoply of programs that were in scope through the various pieces of legislation and how they might work together to efficiently target the impacted communities. These programs included the PUA, EIDL, PPP, and eventually industry-focused assistance for restaurants and certain public facilities known as the Restaurant Revitalization Fund and the Shuttered Venues Operators Grant, respectively.[60] Working across government and alongside private sector partners and nonprofits, could the agency tie all of this together into a usable framework in time? As one commentator noted, "*The SBA had an impossible job and they did it pretty well.*" Another added, "*It's been around for over 50 years, but oftentimes it was kind of the redheaded stepchild. People treated SBA as kind of a lender of last resort, and I just don't think that's necessarily the*

60 "*Congress created two sector-specific SBA programs to target aid to venue operators and food services businesses. The Shuttered Venue Operators Grant program, established in 2020 by the Consolidated Appropriations Act, 2021, and amended by the American Rescue Plan Act, includes over $16 billion in grants to shuttered venues. The Restaurant Revitalization Fund, established in 2021 by the American Rescue Plan Act, provides funding to restaurants and other food service establishments to compensate for pandemic-related revenue losses. Businesses eligible for these programs generally fall into the accommodation and food services and arts, entertainment, and recreation sectors. Businesses that chose to receive both a PPP loan in Phase 3 and a Shuttered Venue Operators Grant had the amount of their PPP loan deducted from their Shuttered Venue Operators Grant award.*" (From *Paycheck Protection Program: Program Changes Increased Lending to the Smallest Businesses and in Underserved Locations*, US Government Accountability Office report to Congress, September 2021, https://www.gao.gov/assets/gao-21-601.pdf.)

case anymore.... I think there's a huge opportunity for SBA to take the goodwill that they've gained over the last couple years and really try to help more small businesses and really shine."[61]

But of course, the agency did not do it alone. Nor was it the only one subject to external criticism. As far as the role of large financial lenders during PPP loan distribution, there were critiques that national banks prioritized their existing clients, thereby forcing out other non-client small businesses from the opportunity to participate in the program. And while those banks balanced a host of issues with this decisioning, including concerns over the ability to vet unknown parties on an expedited basis and other regulatory uncertainties, the distribution of billions of dollars happened in relatively short order. Take, for example, Bank of America (BoA), which dispersed over $50 billion in PPP funding during the second quarter of 2020 to become the top small business lender in the United States during that time.[62]

According to BoA Head of Business Banking Sharon Miller, the bank attributed its success to repurposing staff to a ten-thousand-member support team alongside a multibillion-dollar technology spend in advance of the COVID-19 pandemic; and within forty-five days, it processed what would have normally been eighteen years of small business loans.[63] Organizations like BoA,

---

61 See comments of Michael Brauneis, Protiviti Managing Director, in "PPP 2 Years Later: Analyzing the Legacy and Impact of the $800B Government Relief Program," Anna Hrushka, Banking Dive, May 4, 2022, https://www.bankingdive.com/news/PPP-SBA-small-business-lending-banks-analyzing-legacy-impact-800b-paycheck-protection-program/623160/

62 "How Bank of America's Small-Business Strategy Laid Groundwork for PPP Efforts," Suman Bhattacharyya, Banking Dive, December 8, 2020, https://www.bankingdive.com/news/bank-of-america-coronavirus-paycheck-protection-program/591791/

63 "How Bank of America's Small-Business Strategy Laid Groundwork for PPP Efforts," Bhattacharyya

and so many others, have now proven that when faced with such extreme challenges, they can innovate accordingly. According to Ms. Miller, "*The focus now is on how we help business owners to continue to think about their model, be nimble, and be able to pivot when necessary because any crisis is going to bring opportunity, and we want to be there to have this discussion and be a partner.*"[64]

While the federal government knew that bank lenders would be critical to this effort, mostly out of the pure necessity to distribute the PPP funds quickly, for the first time, the SBA engaged with numerous financial technology firms ("fintechs") to participate in its loan-making efforts. The agency had been reticent to incorporate many of these lenders into its flagship programs for a whole host of oversight, fraud, cyber, and other regulatory risk concerns; however, the circumstances simply accelerated the need for these digital financial services, which has affected that sector in both positive and negative ways.[65] Already significantly impactful in the financial services industry, the SBA was simply left with little choice about fintech involvement if it wanted to ensure that funds got to where they needed to go under a timeline that would keep people employed.

With so many people unable to go to banks in person due to the social conditions, these digital solutions were front and center and will likely continue to deepen their customer access through innovation and traditional bank partnerships. New customer bases have presented opportunities for financial inclusion, allowing traditionally underserved communities and businesses to

64 "How Bank of America's Small-Business Strategy Laid Groundwork for PPP Efforts," Bhattacharyya

65 "The Impact of COVID-19 on Fintech and Its Long-Term Effects," Finance Magnates, April 26, 2023, https://www.financemagnates.com/fintech/payments/the-impact-of-COVID-19-on-fintech-and-its-long-term-effects/

access the financial system. Partnerships with traditional banks have also presented regulatory opportunities, allowing these fintechs to participate in multiple jurisdictions. Notwithstanding these benefits, their susceptibility to fraudulent actors became a significant concern during their PPP involvement. In fact, a report from the US House Select Subcommittee on the Coronavirus Crisis estimated fintechs "*handled 75 percent of the approved PPP loans that had been connected to fraud by DOJ, despite arranging just 15 percent of PPP loans overall at that point,*" and that "*one out of every three PPP loans funded in 2021…failed to implement systems capable of consistently detecting and preventing fraudulent and otherwise ineligible PPP applications.*"[66]

But the large banks and fintechs were by no means alone in the distribution of the PPP funds. Among the most important local economic first responders to this crisis were community banks, minority depository institutions (MDIs), credit unions, and community development financial institutions (CDFIs). Notwithstanding the massive distribution impact that traditional banks ultimately had on the PPP, some have pointed to large-bank apprehensions over a lack of clarity on the rules in the initial program rollout, as well as concerns over private lawsuits and the relatively recent regulatory trauma associated with the Great Recession, as reasons for an initial delay in their borrower outreach.[67] In fact, in early May 2020, the *American Banker* shared

66 "'We are Not the Fraud Police': How Fintechs Facilitated Fraud in the Paycheck Protection Program," US House Select Subcommittee on the Coronavirus Crisis hearing, December 2022, https://coronavirus-democrats-oversight.house.gov/sites/democrats.coronavirus.house.gov/files/2022.12.01%20How%20Fintechs%20Facilitated%20Fraud%20in%20the%20Paycheck%20Protection%20Program.pdf

67 "The Job Preservation Effects of Paycheck Protection Program Loans," Faulkender, Jackman, and Miran

that "*[g]iven the uncertainties surrounding the PPP, banks need both better guidance and more reassurance from the financial regulators. Otherwise, the ghosts of 2008 could continue to haunt bankers as they try to carry out government policy at a perilous moment in the nation's economic history.*"[68]

In the alternative, it seemed that many of the other authorized financial institutions sought to jump right in. While it may be fair to opine that these groups may have entered this arena so aggressively due to their hyper local community relationships, some have argued that the reason they made PPP loans so quickly was in part because their concerns over regulatory scrutiny were simply not as significant as their large-bank counterparts.[69] Ultimately, the community banks, MDIs, and CDFIs were key lenders for underserved communities. In fact, community banks accounted for nearly 60 percent of total lending with an average household income of less than $40,000, over 70 percent to both minority-owned and veteran-owned businesses, and 80 percent to women-owned businesses.[70]

The importance of these loans to the most underserved areas cannot be overstated. For example, over three hundred CDFIs

68 "The Job Preservation Effects of Paycheck Protection Program Loans," Faulkender, Jackman, and Miran

69 "The Job Preservation Effects of Paycheck Protection Program Loans," Faulkender, Jackman, and Miran

70 "An Empirical Review of the Paycheck Protection Program," hearing before US House Committee on Small Business Subcommittee on Oversight, Investigations and Regulations, March 16, 2022, https://docs.house.gov/Committee/Calendar/ByEvent.aspx?EventID=114490; Testimony of Robert J. Barnes, President and CEO of Priority One Bank, on behalf of the Independent Community Bankers of America, during hearing on "An Empirical Review of the Paycheck Protection Program," March 16, 2022, https://www.icba.org/docs/default-source/icba/advocacy-documents/testimony/testimony-on-sba-and-ppp.pdf?sfvrsn=d3c91917_0

made nearly $7.5 billion in loans in the first ninety days of the program, with a final tally of approximately $16 billion in PPP loans.[71] This may not seem like much given the overall size of the program, but consider that the collective community of CDFIs not only pales in comparison to the available resources and personnel of the large banks but they also held less than 1 percent of the assets of the other PPP lending banks and credit unions.[72] And approximately 70 percent of this lending went to low-income areas and minority communities, as compared to just over 20 percent of traditional bank lending.[73] Senator Rubio referred to the efforts of the MDIs and CDFIs as "heroic," stating "*the capital lent by CDFIs and Minority Depository Institutions through PPP was more than the total amount of capital guaranteed by the government during the last decade through these programs combined*."[74]

In fact, as mentioned, by the end of the final phase of PPP lending, the percentage of funds to these undeserved communities was commensurate to their overall small business representation, much of which was due to responsive bipartisan program

---

71 "Update from CFI Fund Director Jodie Harris: CDFI Fund Expands Target Market Eligibility for Payroll Protection Program Lending," US Department of the Treasury Community Development Financial Institutions Fund, December 9, 2020, https://www.cdfifund.gov/news/402

72 "These Community Banking Institutions Should Be at the Center of the Recovering Economy, Chris Pilkerton, Fast Company, June 18, 2021, https://www.fastcompany.com/90648212/these-community-banking-institutions-should-be-the-center-of-the-recovering-economy

73 "New York CDFI Delivers Pandemic Relief to Family-Owned Business," US Department of the Treasury Community Development Financial Institutions Fund, April 20, 2023, https://www.cdfifund.gov/impact/101

74 "Rubio Statement on Biden Administration Changes to Paycheck Protection Program," US Senator Marco Rubio, press release, February 22, 2021, https://www.rubio.senate.gov/rubio-statement-on-biden-administration-changes-to-paycheck-protection-program/

changes to the PPP, including the $10 billion set-aside in May 2020 and an exclusive lending window in a later phase of the program.[75] Secretary Mnuchin publicly highlighted that bipartisan effort "*to ensure that traditionally underserved communities have every opportunity to emerge from the pandemic stronger than before.*"[76] And these circumstances may have presented a blueprint for how CDFIs in particular can scale beyond pandemic circumstances, as many states have since engaged in public-private partnerships to identify both government and private sector capital to be lent directly through these organizations that are already connected to these communities, as demonstrated by their PPP impact.[77]

While so much was happening at the federal and state level, cities sought to step up and do their part to address the needs of their residents. Over the course of the COVID-19 pandemic, small businesses experienced deep double-digit percentages of lost revenue, reduced budgets, wage cuts, and closures; however, in the midst of all of this, surveys show that almost half of them embraced digital and regulatory innovations.[78] Cities adapted local ordinances to challenging economic environments by relaxing and/or fast-tracking permitting processes to make construction activity easier, allowing restaurants to engage in curb-

75 *Paycheck Protection Program: Program Changes Increased Lending to the Smallest Businesses*, US Government Accountability Office report

76 "SBA and Treasury Set Aside $10 Billion for CDFIs to Participate in PPP," Insider NJ, May, 28, 2020, https://www.insidernj.com/press-release/SBA-treasury-set-aside-10-billion-cdfis-participate-PPP/

77 For examples, see the following programs: California Rebuilding Fund, https://ibank.ca.gov/small-business/california-rebuilding-fund/; Southern Opportunity and Resilience Fund, https://calvertimpact.org/investing/soar-fund

78 "2021 Small Business Trends, A Look at the State of Small Business in 2021," Guidant Financial, https://www.guidantfinancial.com/2021-small-business-trends/

side pickup and delivery, and advancing innovations through online sales and e-commerce markets. [79] The White House had daily engagement with local mayors and economic development officials. Some were confident that they could figure out ways to actively work with the federal government and marshal their own resources to creatively support the needs across their communities, but many other local leaders were understandably overwhelmed, looking for any kind of best practices they could duplicate to help support their citizenry.

And some small business innovators not only modified their activities in real time but also did so to the direct benefit of the American people. Not unlike the machine factories of World War II that pivoted production to support the war effort, during the COVID-19 pandemic, some small businesses took the patriotic turn of developing much-needed public health supplies to support the US stockpile, while creating products and services that would enhance their businesses to keep people employed. Take, for example, the many textile companies in North Carolina.[80] That state had lost more than 330,000 manufacturing jobs between 2000 and 2010, and the COVID-19 pandemic only added to those numbers, as factories continued to close across the region.[81] However, people like Andy Warlick, CEO of yarn and cotton manufacturer Parkdale Mills of Gastonia, North Carolina, saw opportunity amid these challenges to create masks and med-

---

79 "Crisis Legislation: Analyzing the Noble Quest of the Paycheck Protection Program to Save Small Businesses," Patrick D. N. Perkins, *Nebraska Law Review*, vol. 101, no. 4, 2022, https://digitalcommons.unl.edu/nlr/vol101/iss4/4

80 "Some N.C. Manufacturers Find a Lifeline in Protective Equipment," Virginia Annable, Government Technology, July 24, 2020, https://www.govtech.com/em/safety/some-nc-manufacturers-find-a-lifeline-in-protective-equipment-.html

81 "Some N.C. Manufacturers Find a Lifeline in Protective Equipment," Annable

ical gear for both retail and government purchase—and Parkdale Mills was not alone.[82]

Executive Director of North Carolina State University Industry Expansion Solutions Phil Mintz shared, "*They [small business manufacturers] all were very willing to jump in and help out and many of them did. Some for regular survival—they saw an opportunity to maintain their staff. Others just wanted to help out.*"[83] This once vibrant American industry was gutted by globalization in previous decades, but incubating models, like Catawba Valley Community College's Manufacturing Solutions Center and Gaston College's Textile Technology Center, invigorated domestic advanced manufacturing across the state, including the production of much-needed diagnostic kits, shields, and protective gowns during the pandemic.[84] This not only served as a clear example of the innate ability to strengthen the American domestic supply chain in a time of crisis but also may just have been one giant step toward revitalizing an entire industry. One local official stated, "*The pandemic, hopefully, will end soon, but the ability to produce these products will be here at home, not in the hands of our adversaries. If needed, we will have the ability to produce high-quality PPE to suppress whatever medical threat might emerge. Furthermore, these research and development capabilities will likely allow us to design PPE equipment and items that will evolve into products we cannot imagine presently. We, in the*

---

82 "Some N.C. Manufacturers Find a Lifeline in Protective Equipment," Annable

83 "Some N.C. Manufacturers Find a Lifeline in Protective Equipment," Annable (brackets added)

84 "Partnership Helps Grow CVCC's Manufacturing Solutions Center, Local Industry," Catawba Valley Community College, September 11, 2020, https://www.cvcc.edu/news/Partnership-helps-grow-CVCC-s-Manufacturing-Solutions-Center-local-industry.cfm

Catawba Valley, are innovators, we don't just make things, we make better things! What we see today is just the beginning."[85]

Along with these kinds of innovations, one unique component of the PPP as an SBA-delivered program was that it permitted nonprofits to access the loans—allowing so many of these local organizations to advance their own community engagement and assistance programs during a time of crisis. And while the force multiplier effort of keeping these nonprofits active and engaged is difficult to quantify, the direct operational impact on these organizations was significant. In the face of economic turmoil when donor access could certainly dry up for so many of these groups, by the summer of 2020, the PPP is estimated to have supported as many as a third of nonprofit jobs, with participation rates as high as 67 percent across the states.[86]

For example, noting the fellowship and internal support of their congregations, local houses of worship became critical recipients of these funds. Under standard SBA programs, these organizations typically have had very limited access to small business loans as part of their support programs for traditional disaster circumstances, and even those are typically reserved for situations where non-religious sections of facilities have been damaged (e.g., parking lots). But with access to PPP, local churches, synagogues, and mosques were able to stay open and

85 "Some N.C. Manufacturers Find a Lifeline in Protective Equipment," Annable; "Partnership Helps Grow CVCC's Manufacturing Solutions Center," Catawba Valley Community College

86 "In the Time of Coronavirus: How Many Eligible Nonprofits Benefited from the Paycheck Protection Program?" Jeff Williams, Dorothy A. Johnson Center for Philanthropy, July 21, 2020, https://johnsoncenter.org/blog/in-the-time-of-coronavirus-how-many-eligible-nonprofits-benefited-from-the-paycheck-protection-program/

provide important assistance to their congregants and communities, supporting food banks, job fairs, and other much-needed functions. That said, it has been reported that this novel funding access permitted loans to be made to so-called megachurches, which may have already had sufficient financial resources to weather the impacts of the COVID-19 pandemic.[87] While there may be merit to this analysis, there is no denying that giving access to these smaller organizations in particular, and so many other impactful nonprofits, allowed them to provide critical services to folks who had nowhere else to turn in the midst of shutdowns and economic frailty.

In many ways, and through a myriad of criticisms, the PPP has been hailed as a success. But how does that kind of success hold up against the lens of Dr. Osler?

Just before the turn of the twentieth century, Dr. Osler gave a graduation speech at the University of Minnesota in which he shared that success in medicine required "*the art of detachment, the virtue of method, the quality of thoroughness, and the grace of humility*."[88] To the first point, he stressed the need to love your fellow man but not be too overly emotionally connected to the people you serve.[89] Focusing on the second element, he shared, "*Ask any active business man or a leader in a profession the secret which enables him to accomplish much work, and he will reply in*

87 *William Osler: A Life in Medicine*, Michael Bliss (University of Toronto Press, 1999)

88 "Sir William Osler's 'Influences' for the Successful Physician, A Reappraisal After 126 Years," Segio A. Castillo-Torres, Ingrid E. Estrada, and Andrew J. Lees, *Archives of Medical Research*, vol. 49, no. 6, August 2018, https://www.sciencedirect.com/science/article/abs/pii/S0188440918307550

89 "Sir William Osler's 'Influences' for the Successful Physician," Castillo-Torres, Estrada, and Lees

one word, system."[90] To the third trait of thoroughness, he added, "*A knowledge of the fundamental sciences upon which our art is based...not a smattering, but a full and deep acquaintance, not with all of the facts, that is impossible, but with the great principles based upon them.*"[91] As his final theme, which he shared as among the most critical, he noted, "*Start out with the conviction that absolute truth is hard to reach in matters relating to our fellow creatures...that errors in judgment must occur in the practice of an art which consists largely in balancing probabilities.*"[92]

While many small business owners may never meet them in person, dedicated public servants constructed the PPP program for the benefit of the American people. Although its processes required some changes over time, the PPP provided a critical lifeline for so many by a designed system for loan making and forgiveness. Decisions were made with the best available information, historical precedents, and advice from economic experts amid a scenario where all the health-related impacts were simply unknowable. Finally, it is with humility and sincere reflection that we now undertake this work to ensure we are prepared to defend against the next economic contagion.

Under his definition, I believe Dr. Osler would view the PPP, and the work of so many who built and delivered on it, as a success.

---

90 "Sir William Osler's 'Influences' for the Successful Physician," Castillo-Torres, Estrada, and Lees

91 "Sir William Osler's 'Influences' for the Successful Physician," Castillo-Torres, Estrada, and Lees

92 "Sir William Osler's 'Influences' for the Successful Physician," Castillo-Torres, Estrada, and Lees

CHAPTER FOUR

Real-Time Decision-Making and the Challenges of the PPP Initiative

To study the phenomena of disease without books is to sail an uncharted sea, while to study books without patients is not to go to sea at all.

Dr. Osler is famous for many medical advances, but chief among them is the concept of the "residency," during which newly minted doctors work directly with patients to hone their skills and acumen in a particular field of medicine. Even prior to this, Dr. Osler pioneered patient interaction with medical students while still in school, as his philosophy was that the library of medicine and the practical experience with the patient went hand in hand. This may seem almost mundane in a modern medical context, but for the time it was groundbreaking, and has, of course, become the norm ever since.

The assignment of particular patients, maintenance of daily records, engagement in the associated treatments, and work under the direct supervision of attending faculty physicians were unique to Johns Hopkins during those early years, as were the legendary quizzes that Dr. Osler administered to these students.[1] Failure to answer questions correctly often resulted in the student being sent to his medical library, demonstrating the immutable link between the academic and the practitioner.[2] But Dr. Osler is said to have had a quality about him that was much different than we have seen in the medical dramatizations of popular culture. A former Osler student and ultimately a dean of Harvard Medical School, Henry Christian, once stated, "*His criticisms of students and their work were incisive and unforgettable, but never harsh or unkindly; they inspired respect and affection, never fear.*"[3] Success was, of course, always the goal, but Dr. Osler would also use his own mistakes as examples, noting that "*[e]rrors cannot be avoided,*" and that "*[e]rrors in judgment must occur in the practice of an art which consists largely of balancing probabilities*; surely recognizing that even the most informed physician, and for that matter policymaker, must in part rely on balancing their knowledge and observation with plausible outcomes.[4]

Prior to the COVID-19 pandemic, it was common practice for the hardworking men and women of the US Small Business Administration to engage directly with the millions of small businesses around the country—whether it was through funding, advising, or support for federal contracting opportunities. But while the economic diagnosis at the beginning of the COVID-19

1 *William Osler: A Life in Medicine*, Michael Bliss (University of Toronto Press, 1999)
2 *William Osler: A Life in Medicine*, Bliss
3 *William Osler: A Life in Medicine*, Bliss
4 *The Quotable Osler*, Mark Silverman, T. Jock Murray, and Charles S. Bryan, eds. (American College of Physicians, 2007)

pandemic was so dire that the typical level of direct public engagement became strained, all the staff could do was assess the general state of American small business, acknowledge the tools and operational mechanisms that they had at their disposal, and implement the new innovative authorities that had been granted to them by Congress. The expectation was that those authorities would be applied immediately and without hesitation. The typical process of government is often criticized for being anything but fast, but as emergency circumstances were in place, and even though rules and practices were changing daily, the only thing that truly mattered was to protect as many businesses and jobs as possible.

There are some foundational components of PPP that are irrefutable. First, given the timing of the need, there was no ability for a truly comprehensive material economic needs assessment by Congress prior to release of the first tranche of funds. Due to the unique nature of the circumstances, the economic and legislative approach was seemingly a combination of art and science. And while it was certainly informed by financial expertise, the congressional decision-makers who ultimately voted on the CARES Act were men and women from all walks of life, geographies, and professions. Party politics aside, they had to make their own assessment of the totality of circumstances. Not unlike a physician confronting a patient with a novel disease, they were faced with questions that they simply couldn't answer with complete certainty. Would it work? Was it enough? How much was too much? And would this bill have unintended impacts on their constituents and across the country? Among these dire circumstances and amid these questions, these elected officials had to weigh the fact that the CARES Act and its progeny legislation would have an enormous impact on the federal deficit, as fiscal years 2020 and 2021 presented two of the largest budget deficits since World War II.[5] Not to mention the fact that fraud estimates to date could range in the tens of billions and beyond.[6] All of that said, assessing the patient as best as they could at the time, the House passed the $2 trillion-plus CARES Act by a vote of 419–6 and the Senate approved it by a vote of 96–0.

Even with such overwhelming support, while there were program challenges at the time and serious questions that remained, those that criticize the implementation of the PPP must contend with the argument that without it—warts and all—our small business ecosystem could have very easily been damaged beyond repair. Both political parties knew it would not be perfect, but seemingly the apt cliché that applied here is that *one shouldn't let the perfect be the enemy of the good.* A postmortem assessment of this program is not only necessary from a good government perspective but also critical for the foundations of a future response. Just like the experiences of the famed Dr. Osler, errors cannot be avoided, and those who have lived through such a crisis owe it to the next generation of practitioners to share the wealth of that knowledge.

So, where do we begin in probing a nearly $1 trillion program? Let's start with those 535 decision-makers in Congress. It could be argued that their political infighting took too long, forcing small businesses to make devastating choices of layoffs, closures, and bankruptcies during the earliest days of the COVID-19 pandemic.

---

5 *Federal Deficits, Growing Debt, and the Economy in the Wake of COVID-19*, Congressional Research Service report, March 23, 2021, https://crsreports.congress.gov/product/pdf/R/R46729

6 "SBA Potentially Lost $200 Billion in Covid Pandemic Relief to Fraud and Abuse, Government Watchdog Finds," Ana Faguy, *Forbes*, June 27, 2023, https://www.forbes.com/sites/anafaguy/2023/06/27/sba-lost-200-billion-in-covid-pandemic-relief-to-fraud-and-abuse-government-watchdog-finds/

Notwithstanding such a criticism, the legislative process set forth by the Founding Fathers intended for debate and analysis, and to blame this method somewhat undermines the constitutional structure of the many other necessary policy deliberations envisioned under our democratic system of government. However, as it could certainly be argued that this was, in fact, an emergency of devastating proportions, perhaps it should have taken hours—not days—for the parties to come together with a comprehensive solution. And in theory, from the perspective of those most significantly impacted, that position would have genuine merit. But it does raise the question that if certain decisions must be streamlined, how do we practically account for what decisions those should be? Is it for economic disaster? Is it for war? Should the executive agencies have expanded power in these situations, and at those times, should Congress cede its appropriations duties? These are very serious and arguably dangerous existential questions about the American democracy and constitutional authorities. And yet they are another reason why developing a generally agreed-upon policy blueprint now can help lay out an agreeable framework and facilitate a swift legislative action plan in the future.

And while the timing of passing an appropriation of this size was undeniably historic, Congress was not the only party involved. As previously mentioned, significant execution components of the language of any legislation are often intentionally vague, so that the executive agencies can utilize their existing processes to oversee, operate, and distribute funding and services accordingly. So, to be fair, Congress passes a bill (for better or for worse), and then most of what they can do is oversight, which includes requests for written information, hearings with government witnesses, and of course media interviews—none of which would likely have an immediate impact on the appropriations associated with the program.

So, should one point the proverbial finger at the executive agencies that implement the vision of such a bill? On the topic of the PPP, that conversation would focus largely on the SBA and the Treasury Department. And one of the most common criticisms heard from both lenders and borrowers was around the topic of administrative program clarity. The US Government Accountability Office (GAO), an independent watchdog agency within the federal government, also identified that there was, in fact, confusion in the rollout of the program.[7] The GAO evidenced this position by citing the fact that there were double-digit sets of additional agency guidance documents that were required beyond the initial explanation of the SBA program.[8] Others have sought to buttress this position by citing that there was also limited access to agency technical support amid the need at the outset for a better understanding of what would be required for loan forgiveness and any associated audits.[9]

It is believed that that confusion and uncertainty led to some small businesses either deciding not to take or returning potential funding because the endgame of the potential conditions for forgiveness versus repayment was either unclear or seemingly being altered at any given time; and those businesses did not want to add those potentially detrimental consequences to their already

7 *Paycheck Protection Program: SBA Added Program Safeguards, but Additional Actions Are Needed*, US Government Accountability Office report, July 2021, https://www.gao.gov/assets/gao-21-577.pdf

8 *Paycheck Protection Program: SBA Added Program Safeguards*, US Government Accountability Office report

9 "Crisis Legislation: Analyzing the Noble Quest of the Paycheck Protection Program to Save Small Businesses," Patrick D. N. Perkins, *Nebraska Law Review*, vol. 101, no. 4, 2022, https://digitalcommons.unl.edu/nlr/vol101/iss4/4

devastating reality. In fact, as of May 31, 2020, businesses had returned more than 170,000 PPP loans, totaling approximately $38.5 billion, to which some have attributed to consternation over mixed SBA guidance.[10] The reality is that in almost any government program there is a substantial amount of time to write draft rules, standardize guidance and test operations, and engage in substantive commentary from impacted stakeholders—but of course, that was not available in these circumstances. This led the SBA and the Treasury Department to regularly publish updates in something of a reactionary mode as issues arose, but certainly with the intent of meeting the supportive economic mission of the PPP. Although most policymakers likely foresaw at least some of these challenges, for many politicians, the balance of this recognition among the daily outreach from frustrated constituents was likely difficult, to say the least.

The most common criticism reported in those early days of the PPP was that people just could not get access to the program. And, of course, with small business borrowers engaging directly with these lenders, they would understandably place the blame for any challenges or delays squarely at the feet of the participating financial institutions, including posting concerns on public message boards saying things like, "*The process definitely makes you wonder if they have forgotten you along the way! Step 1 was at 10 a.m. this morning and as of 5 p.m., still waiting for Step 2. Best of luck everyone*," and "*My gut tells me many banks are taking the applications now but waiting until next week to actually process them after the[y] figure out all the parts to the puzzle, etc...but*

10 "More than $38 Billion in PPP Loans for Small Firms Canceled," Mark Niquette, Bloomberg, June 25, 2020, https://www.bloomberg.com/news/articles/2020-06-25/more-than-38-billion-in-ppp-loans-for-small-firms-canceled

what do I know?!?"[11] In the midst of this confusion between lenders and borrowers, notable celebrities engaged in public advice, even famed entrepreneur and *Shark Tank* staple Mark Cuban. CNBC summarized his thoughts when he spoke on the show *Squawk Box*: "*Small businesses should apply to multiple banks to boost their chances of getting a loan.*"[12]

While businesses pointed to confusing statements coming from the lenders themselves, those same financial institutions directed the blame back at the agency. The most illustrative of which was that the initial SBA guidelines were released the night before the program opened, leading to confusion over exactly what loans would qualify, the full application process, and the timing of loan funding.[13] In April 2020, Rob Nichols, CEO of the American Bankers Association (ABA), shared in a social media post that "*[b]anks of all sizes worked through the night to process #PPP loans with little success.*"[14] And this frustration was not just at the national level, as state bankers from Alabama to New Mexico made their concerns public, sharing feedback like "*Just another Friday night where [SBA and Treasury] continue to muddy the forgiveness water to make it as complicated as possible to obtain forgiveness and bankers to manage it.*"[15]

---

11 "PPP – Banks Off to Crawl," Pediatric Management Institute, https://forum.pediatricsupport.com/t/PPP-banks-off-to-crawl/2486

12 *Mark Cuban: Small Business Should Apply to Multiple Banks to Increase Odds of PPP Loan Approval*, CNBC *Squawk Box* video, May 1, 2020, https://www.cnbc.com/video/2020/05/01/mark-cuban-small-businesses-loan-paycheck-protection-program.html#:~:text=Mark%20Cuban%2C%20co%2Dhost%20of,through%20the%20Paycheck%20Protection%20Program

13 "Crisis Legislation: Analyzing the Noble Quest of the Paycheck Protection Program," Perkins

14 "U.S. Banks Battle Technology Issues in Race for $310 Billion in New Small-Business Aid," Michelle Price, Reuters, April 28, 2020, https://www.reuters.com/article/idUSKCN22A2KN/

15 "Survey: 3 in 4 PPP Borrowers Confused by Loan's Terms," Dan Ennis, Banking Dive, May 26, 2020, https://www.bankingdive.com/news/borrowers-paycheck-protection-program-confusion-loan-terms/578577/ (brackets in original)

Even though the federal government did release significant written guidance on the particulars of the program, as well as innumerable explanatory webinars to local chambers of commerce, industry associations, and community action groups; financial and legal advisers continued to share that they were unprepared to properly advise small businesses. And of course, all these complaints around the process assumed an actual awareness of the program, which was, of course, yet another challenge, as researchers have shared that only "*68% of businesses with fewer than five employees reported knowing about government programs…and this share remained below 80% through April 16th, when the PPP exhausted its initial funding*."[16] Daily press conferences were often used at both the federal and state levels to advise Americans of health-related circumstances, and notwithstanding Secretary Mnuchin's periodic involvement in those updates, a comparable centralized approach was not as routinely undertaken on the related economic programs.

One of the reasons for the frustration on the borrower side seems to have been that some financial institutions were serving existing customers before new borrowers, some even being accused of providing "*concierge treatment*" to those borrowers.[17] ABA CEO Rob Nichols conveyed early on that prioritizing existing customers was not in conflict with lender protocols, noting that "*[b]anks of all sizes were always encouraged by the administration to process loans for both new and existing customers at*

16 "Information Frictions and Access to the Paycheck Protection Program," John Eric Humphries, Christopher A. Neilson, and Gabriel Ulyssea, *Journal of Public Economics*, August 21, 2020; available at NIH National Library of Medicine: https://www.ncbi.nlm.nih.gov/pmc/articles/PMC7441872/

17 "Banks Gave Richest Clients 'Concierge Treatment' for Pandemic Aid," Emily Flitter and Stacy Cowley, *New York Times*, April 22, 2020, https://www.nytimes.com/2020/04/22/business/sba-loans-ppp-coronavirus.html

the onset of the PPP program. They were also encouraged to start processing loans as quickly as possible to support the deteriorating economy."[18] It would seem that part of the practical rationale for any perceived prioritization would be due to the fact that the banks already had the critical identification and business information about their existing clients on record, making it easier to process their PPP applications and get loans out the door—which, of course, was the intended program role of the lenders. From a required fraud-check perspective, the banks already *knew* these customers via the standard anti-money laundering assessments conducted upon any bank account opening. And with those relationships in place, some of those early loans may have been transacted through personal small business bankers, and as reported, once the program design became clearer, more comprehensive bank engagement followed suit.[19]

However, an analysis that has been presented of the perceived preference by larger banks is that by supporting their own customers first, those businesses would of course be able to remain current on any other debts, ensuring the strength of the lending institution's overall balance sheet and the so-called stickiness of those customers to the financial institution.[20] Whether or not that actually factored into any calculation, the banks undoubtedly played a major role in getting PPP funds out into the economy, but the criticisms remain that the PPP design did not properly incentivize these financial institutions to proactively engage with

---

18 "Treasury Encouraged Banks to Prioritize PPP Loans for Existing Clients, Hurting Minority- and Women-Owned Small Businesses, House Report Says," Hannah Miao, CNBC, October 16, 2020, https://www.cnbc.com/2020/10/16/treasury-encouraged-banks-to-prioritize-PPP-loans-for-existing-clients.html

19 "Treasury Encouraged Banks to Prioritize PPP Loans for Existing Clients," Miao

20 "Banks Gave Richest Clients 'Concierge Treatment,'" Flitter and Cowley

businesses that had more traditionally limited access to the banking sector.[21] A follow-on congressional assessment of this issue opined that this reality likely had a more significant impact on the small businesses ecosystem, citing that, as a result, "*[s]mall businesses that were truly in need of financial support during the economic crisis often faced longer waits and more obstacles to receiving PPP funding than larger, wealthier companies.*"[22] Regardless, notwithstanding the "*first-come, first-served*" approach set forth in the regulatory guidance, the fact still remains that some smaller firms did not access the program in those early days of the PPP; but it should be noted that along with the claim of prioritization, some researchers allocate at least a portion of this issue to what has been referred to as "funding hesitancy." [23] And while there were few, if any, realistic alternatives to the PPP to achieve the goals of speed and distribution, this term is meant to explain that certain small businesses—particularly those without banking relationships—may have been reluctant to participate initially due to concerns over program components such as eligibility, administrative costs, clawbacks, or unforeseen audit expenses.[24]

---

21 "Crisis Legislation: Analyzing the Noble Quest of the Paycheck Protection Program," Perkins

22 "House Report: Treasury Dept. Encouraged Banks to Prioritize Existing Clients for PPP Loans," Jessica Smith, Yahoo, October 16, 202, https://finance.yahoo.com/news/house-report-treasury-dept-encouraged-banks-to-prioritize-existing-clients-for-ppp-loans-182031801.html

23 Testimony of Manju Puri, J. B. Fuqua Professor of Finance, Fuqua School of Business, Duke University, before the US House Committee on Small Business Subcommittee on Oversight, Investigations and Regulations hearing on "An Empirical Review of the Paycheck Protection Program," March 16, 2022; "Information Frictions and Access to the Paycheck Protection Program," Humphries, Neilson, and Ulyssea

24 *CARES Act Assistance for Employers and Employees – The Paycheck Protection Program, Employee Retention Tax Credit, and Unemployment Insurance Benefits: Overview (Part 1),* Congressional Research Service report, April 21, 2020, https://crsreports.congress.gov/product/pdf/IN/IN11324/3; "Information Frictions and Access to the Paycheck Protection Program," Humphries, Neilson, and Ulyssea

Some institutions, like PNC Bank, sought to address this concern head-on, stating that they "*took special care to help ensure that applications from small businesses located in LMI [low-to-moderate income communities] and non-profits were not left behind, as we recognize that those businesses and communities face special challenges and that non-profits often support vulnerable communities.*"[25] That said, the evidence demonstrates that underserved communities faced program challenges, particularly during the early days of the PPP. For example, while studies have shown a significant disparity as to the rates that black-owned businesses obtained full funding (43 percent) versus white-owned businesses (80 percent), the identified divide has also been shown to be economic in nature.[26] Setting aside race and looking squarely at the financial data, MIT Professor David Autor and his colleagues argue that nearly 75 percent of PPP loans were received by the top economic quartile of Americans among a more equitable distribution of unemployment insurance and household stimulus support, which is juxtaposed against studies that show that the impact of unemployment insurance on these same communities may have been as low as 20 percent.[27] While this data does

---

25 "House Report: Treasury Dept. Encouraged Banks to Prioritize Existing Clients for PPP Loans," Smith

26 "The $800 Billion Paycheck Protection Program: Where Did the Money Go and Why Did It Go There?" David Autor, David Cho, Leland D. Crane, Mita Goldar, Byron Lutz, Joshua Montes, William B. Peterman, David Ratner, Daniel Villar, and Ahu Yildirmaz, National Bureau of Economic Research, January 2022, https://www.nber.org/system/files/working_papers/w29669/w29669.pdf; "Crisis Legislation: Analyzing the Noble Quest of the Paycheck Protection Program," Perkins

27 "The $800 Billion Paycheck Protection Program," Autor et al.; "Was the Paycheck Protection Program Effective?" William R. Emmons and Drew Dahl, Federal Reserve Bank of St. Louis, July 6, 2022, https://www.stlouisfed.org/publications/regional-economist/2022/jul/was-paycheck-protection-program-effective#:~:text=The%20PPP%20was%20a%20very,of%20the%20COVID-19%2D19%20crisis

appear to identify a design flaw that can and must certainly be cured in the future, in fairness, it should be viewed in the context of the concern over funding hesitancy in order to ensure that any such remedy also accounts for wide and fulsome distribution of such critical information about program access.

All of this said, it should be noted that interview findings presented to the House Oversight Subcommittee examining these issues indicated that they "*did not confirm biases by lenders or the SBA against minority- or female-owned businesses*," but rather any appearance of unequal treatment focused on the loan size of under $150,000 as opposed to demographics of the borrower.[28] While there are multiple ways to address this access disparity in future pandemics, and many lenders such as community banks, MDIs, CDFIs, credit unions, and to a certain extent fintechs, sought to fill that breach, this line of analysis points to the harsh reality that communities that were economically vulnerable before the COVID-19 pandemic likely became even more so once it began. [29]

That said, the federal government took multiple steps to address some of these issues during the course of the COVID-19 pandemic, including the admission of approximately six hundred new lenders in the second phase of PPP, which comprised more community-based lenders and fintechs, in order to reach impact goals of proportional lending to underserved communi-

28 Testimony of Dr. Iryna Demko, Research Associate, Center for Economic Development, Maxine Goodman Levin College of Urban Affairs, Cleveland State University, before the US House Committee on Small Business Subcommittee on Oversight, Investigations and Regulations hearing on "An Empirical Review of the Paycheck Protection Program," March 16, 2022

29 "Small Businesses and Government Assistance During COVID-19: Evidence from the PPP in the U.S.," Qingfang Wang and Wei Kang, Sage Journals, April 3, 2023, https://orcid.org/0000-0002-7285-4027

ties.[30] Alongside the admission for more lenders, many of which maintained a very local lending footprint, the aforementioned $10 billion set-aside was put into place to better support underserved and minority-owned businesses.[31] While these changes certainly made a difference, it points to important policy considerations for addressing lending disparities not just in pandemic circumstances but perhaps in normal conditions as well, including the potential need for more awareness and alignment in access to training, technical assistance, financial education, and business planning.[32]

But beyond just the condemnations of existing customer prioritization and limitations on lending to underserved communities, the program has also been criticized for challenges associated with getting the funds to companies that truly needed the cash to survive. To understand this a bit better, the reader may need a brief primer on SBA rules around what is referred to as "affiliation" and "credit elsewhere." In short, these two concepts are commonly used components of any SBA loan program to ensure that the traditional SBA-backed small business loan goes to independently owned and operated small businesses that need this unique government support, and does not serve as a subsidy program for larger corporations that presumably already have ample resources, acting as a competitive advantage to smaller entities.[33] So, for example, in the case of a national franchise restaurant, the

30 *Paycheck Protection Program: Program Changes Increased Lending to the Smallest Businesses and in Underserved Locations*, US Government Accountability Office report to Congress, September 2021, https://www.gao.gov/assets/gao-21-601.pdf

31 *Paycheck Protection Program: Program Changes Increased Lending to the Smallest Businesses*, US Government Accountability Office report

32 "Small Businesses and Government Assistance during COVID-19," Wang and Kang

33 "Paycheck Protection Program (PPP) Information Sheet: Borrowers," https://home.treasury.gov/system/files/136/PPP--Fact-Sheet.pdf

SBA wants to ensure that the success of the business is dependent on the individual small business owner, including traditional management decisions, like hiring/firing, etc. While these stores may share the brand name, logos, and certain operational standards, for access to SBA-backed funding, they should be separately owned, with key decision-making authority maintained and executed by the small business owners themselves. In these circumstances, SBA made the determinations that if this business had not ceded this authority to a franchisor, these businesses are in fact small and are not affiliated with a larger operation, thereby allowing them access to traditional SBA lending. If the key company decisions were made at a corporate level—at a public company or otherwise—under the affiliation rule analysis, it would cease to be a small business under both the legislative intent and the actual verbiage of SBA's 1953 authorizing statute, in that they do not truly stand on their own.[34]

This affiliation concept goes hand in hand with the "credit elsewhere" concept, in that if the business can get access to credit via some other means—a market-based bank loan or a private equity investment, for example—it would not necessarily be a responsible use of taxpayer money to provide a government-backed guarantee in the traditional capitalist marketplace.[35] However, with these two foundational components of SBA lending removed for PPP loans, the voices of trade associations and public critics reached a fever pitch. Public companies that traded on a national stock exchange and businesses owned wholly or in part by private

34 "Paycheck Protection Program (PPP) Information Sheet: Borrowers," https://home.treasury.gov/system/files/136/PPP--Fact-Sheet.pdf

35 "Paycheck Protection Program (PPP) Information Sheet: Borrowers," https://home.treasury.gov/system/files/136/PPP--Fact-Sheet.pdf

equity firms, among others, applied for and received PPP loans. And regardless of their legal merit under the rules of the program, many of these loans were criticized as unnecessary, taking advantage of the system, and exhausting funding for the intended recipient communities.

Within the first two weeks of the program launch, it was discovered that perhaps over ninety loans were made to publicly traded companies and their subsidiaries, totaling $365 million.[36] Media scrutiny was particularly impactful here due to the widely publicized distribution of stories of PPP loans going to such recognizable organizations as the Los Angeles Lakers, valued at almost $4 billion and which received a nearly $5 million loan, or a $10 million PPP loan going to well-known hamburger chain Shake Shack, valued at $1.6 billion with eight thousand employees.[37] Alongside a slew of other recipients that also presumably had meaningful capital access elsewhere, once the identities of these publicly traded firms were released, many of them voluntarily decided to repay the PPP loan proceeds they had received. While it is unclear if those initial applications were technically illegal given the rules in place at the time, these repayments were likely in their own public relations interest. However, Secretary Mnuchin did announce in late April 2020 that there may be criminal liability in play, stating that he encouraged "*everybody to look at this and pay back these loans now so we can recycle the money if*

36 "These Publicly Traded Companies Took Millions in PPP Loan Money," Chris Morris, *Fortune*, April 22, 2020, https://fortune.com/2020/04/22/small-business-loans-ppp-public-companies-coronavirus-stimulus-cares-act-sba/

37 "The Los Angeles Lakers' $4.6 Million Loan was 'Outrageous,' Treasury Secretary Says as the Team Returns Money Meant for Small Businesses," Graham Rapier, Business Insider, April 28, 2020, https://www.businessinsider.com/los-angeles-lakers-small-business-PPP-loan-outrageous-steven-mnuchin-2020-4

you made a mistake."[38] Thereafter, SBA issued formal direction to address this issue in its "Frequently Asked Questions" guidance, which stated:

> *Question: Do businesses owned by large companies with adequate sources of liquidity to support the business's ongoing operations qualify for a PPP loan?*
>
> *Answer: [Pertinent part copied here] [B]orrowers still must certify in good faith that their PPP loan request is necessary…taking into account their current business activity and their ability to access other sources of liquidity sufficient to support their ongoing operations in a manner that is not significantly detrimental to the business. For example, it is unlikely that a public company with substantial market value and access to capital markets will be able to make the required certification in good faith*."

The general guidance was that "*businesses that are now uncertain as to their eligibility under the new SBA guidance should consider whether they should withdraw their PPP loan application, and those that have received a PPP loan already may want to consider repaying their loan by May 7, 2020, to take advantage of the good faith certification safe-harbor under the new guidance*."[39]

---

38 "Crisis Legislation: Analyzing the Noble Quest of the Paycheck Protection Program," Perkins; "Mnuchin Warns of 'Criminal Liability' for Public Companies Taking Small Business Loans," Sergei K. Lebnikov, *Forbes*, April 28, 2020, https://www.forbes.com/sites/sergeiklebnikov/2020/04/28/mnuchin-warns-of-criminal-liability-for-public-companies-taking-small-business-loans/

39 "Paycheck Protection Program Loans, Frequently Asked Questions," US Small Business Administration fact sheet, June 13, 2003, https://www.sba.gov/sites/default/files/2021-01/Paycheck-Protection-Program-Frequently-Asked-Questions.pdf

A somewhat related criticism involving the original intention of the PPP was that even if the money did go to a truly small business, it was not necessarily the workers that were the true beneficiaries of these funds—but rather the businesses themselves—as the operational portion of the funds went to creditors, landlords, and other third parties.[40] While there were certainly larger parties in the business chain that were not designated as being in direct scope for this particular support (e.g., perhaps a large commercial real estate firm receiving small business rent payments), this criticism is questionable at its core in that this program was intended to keep workers connected to their employers so that they could ultimately return to that job after the crisis had passed, and in order for those businesses to remain viable, payment obligations like these were simply contractually required, absent any negotiated accommodation or emergency ordinance to the contrary.[41] In the identified instance, for example, the federal government could have sought to suspend all commercial rents and other related debts. But there is a fine line between stimulus and overreach, and while personal tenant protections were ultimately enacted by governments, to do so on the commercial side would arguably have created a questionable legal and economic paradigm.

Finally, given the varied impacts of the COVID-19 pandemic, there were additional professional communities that were unable to operate safely, which opened the discussion of targeted assistance to certain other groups. While independent contractors and gig workers did in fact have technical access to

40 "Was the Paycheck Protection Program Effective?" Emmons and Dahl

41 "The $800 Billion Paycheck Protection Program," Autor et al.

unemployment insurance, given its novelty, process questions and procedural limitations of the state unemployment insurance systems were ever-present.[42] Given the significant changes to the US workforce over the previous decade and the rise of company models like Uber, Lyft, and Etsy, it will be very important to account for this growing business demographic in any future pandemic. The sheer scope of this population accounts for a significant portion of working-age adults and is expected to grow exponentially in the future, so responsible future policy models to support these individuals under emergency circumstances should be considered now.

While this list of complications is likely not exhaustive, it serves to demonstrate that there were in fact obstacles throughout the application and disbursement process of the PPP. And while these may be viewed through the eyes of the rational policy professional as challenges, they should be embraced as lessons. Dr. Osler once shared that "*the results of specialized observation are at best only partial truths, which require to be corrected with facts obtained by wider study*." [43] Once again, his words apply to the PPP. The medical and economic calamities that so many faced during the COVID-19 pandemic were heartbreaking, and we know that for so many, those challenges are still very much a part of their lives. But as his opening quote for this chapter illus-

---

42 "More on Unemployment Benefits for the Self-Employed, Independent Contractors and Gig-Economy Workers: Lawyer on Front Lines Answers Advanced Questions," Bruce Brumberg, JD, *Forbes*, May 6, 2020, https://www.forbes.com/sites/brucebrumberg/2020/05/06/more-on-unemployment-benefits-for-the-self-employed-independent-contractors-and-gig-economy-workers-lawyer-on-front-lines-answers-advanced-questions/

43 "William Osler Said," Remedy, Medium, https://medium.com/@Remedy_health/william-osler-said-88cf9fed2866

trates, it is incumbent upon us to do the academic research and analysis now and take any future strategy out of a specialized academic laboratory and into the public, so it can be openly discussed, debated, and pressure-tested before it must be launched as a vessel in real time.

CHAPTER FIVE

Economic Impact of Pandemic on Cities and States

Listen to your patient, he is telling you the diagnosis.

CERTAIN AUTHORITIES ON DR. OSLER share that some of his attributable quotations, or "Oslerisms," can be a challenge to document, and the above statement falls into that category.[1] But aside from its provenance, this phrase is core to Dr. Osler's philosophy. He expands on this idea a bit more when he shares that "*the student begins with the patient, continues with the patient, and ends his studies with the patient, using books and lectures as tools, as means to an end ... Every patient you see is a lesson in much more than the malady from which he suffers*."[2] The style of open-ended questions to a patient discussed earlier, in the example of Dr. Fitzgerald's questioning of the women who had been aboard the *Titanic*, was particularly critical during his time, given the limits on common imaging technologies used during that period.[3]

1 *Osler for White Coat Pockets, A Vade Mecum for Medical Students and Residents*, Joseph B. VanderVeer, MD, and Charles Bryan, MD, American Osler Society (Masthof Press, 2017)

2 *Osler for White Coat Pockets*, VanderVeer and Bryan

3 *Osler for White Coat Pockets*, VanderVeer and Bryan

While many physicians begin with this approach of question and answer, some research has shown that they often cut the patients off within an average of twelve seconds.[4] Assuredly, it is difficult for the experienced and trained professional not to move to diagnosis quickly—particularly if the symptoms resemble something he or she has seen many times before; however, Dr. Osler believed that that interruption of the patient could lead to missing the critical information necessary for a complete diagnosis, not just because it isn't solicited, but because at that point, the patient may choose to limit the information that could have been shared.[5]

While real-time data for the US small business community and its workforce is difficult to obtain, the Federal Reserve conducts an annual survey report, which looks back to the prior year. The report conducted for the 2020 cycle shared worrying information, some of which was, of course, known by policy experts, but it illustrates the need for a consistent and contemporaneous methodology that gives the small business patient a voice for future policy diagnoses and decisioning.[6] The small business respondents in the survey shared that almost all of them had been impacted by the COVID-19 pandemic, and over half expected their revenues to drop by over 25 percent in 2020.[7] Of the 80 percent of firms that experienced financial challenges, over 60 percent used personal funds to fill the gaps, with 55 percent cutting staff and downsizing operations.[8] Well over half of the respondents either reduced

4 *Osler for White Coat Pockets*, VanderVeer and Bryan

5 *Osler for White Coat Pockets*, VanderVeer and Bryan

6 *2021 Report on Employer Firms: Based on the 2020 Small Business Credit Survey*, Federal Reserve Banks small-business credit survey, https://doi.org/10.55350/sbcs-20210203

7 *2021 Report on Employer Firms*, Federal Reserve Banks

8 *2021 Report on Employer Firms*, Federal Reserve Banks

or stop taking a salary altogether, and debt levels increased significantly, with almost half of respondents owing more than $100,000.[9]

Disease, debt, fear, and financial uncertainty—that paints the picture of what many Americans across the small business community experienced throughout 2020. And as one expands out to the local economies, states were also under massive financial pressures, cutting spending due to either balanced budget requirements or other lending mandates. And as might be expected, the impacts of municipal budget shortfalls, coupled with lockdowns and supply chain disruptions, were even more severe across urban port cities of entry in places like Atlanta, Baltimore, Boston, New Orleans, and New York. Their landing locations and high density, combined with the airborne illness, was a recipe for spread of the COVID-19 virus.[10] Very early on, cities such as Atlanta were under initial lockdown, and the government established a COVID-19 hazard pay regimen for local employees.[11] Alongside this unique program, the city eliminated fares for public transportation and established a multimillion-dollar fund to support impacted communities; whereas localities within Ohio, for example, created grant programs for commercial rent reimbursements and coordinated a community program that included payments to restaurants in need of support services.[12]

And while e-commerce was certainly significant before the COVID-19 pandemic, this sector surged while folks worked and

9 *2021 Report on Employer Firms*, Federal Reserve Banks

10 "Edward Glaeser on the Survival of Cities," Betsy Gardner, Data-Smart City Solutions, June 14, 2023, https://datasmart.hks.harvard.edu/edward-glaeser-survival-cities

11 *What COVID-19 Means for City Finances*, National League of Cities report, 2020, https://covid19.nlc.org/wp-content/uploads/2020/06/What-Covid-19-Means-For-City-Finances_Report-Final.pdf

12 *What COVID-19 Means for City Finances*, National League of Cities report

studied from within the confines of their own homes.[13] In fact, from the period of 2019 to 2020, online sales went from $571.2 billion to $815.4 billion.[14] But this massive increase in one sector demonstrated huge changes in others. For example, while stay-at-home protocols were a significant advantage for online retailers, gas station sales went from $513.5 billion to $428.1 billion in that same period, as fewer commuters needed to take to the roads.[15] And, of course, with so much being delivered to front doors, brick-and-mortar retailers saw huge losses without that in-person traffic, coupled with fewer people in a physical office or attending social gatherings for which products like new clothes might have been purchased in previous years. Even as things began to open back up, consumers remained in this e-commerce purchasing mindset, and with other headwinds such as supply chain challenges and staffing shortages, many stores were forced to innovate to attract in-store traffic with parties, refreshments, and door prizes.[16]

Much of this inactivity at the local commerce level led to the predictable impact on state government tax revenues, which fell by 29 percent in the second quarter of 2020.[17] And certain federal resources were stretched as well. In fact, not only did the Internal Revenue Service face substantial delays in return processing, public requests for assistance skyrocketed during the period from 2019 to 2021, in which taxpayer correspondence tripled to an inventory

---

13 "E-Commerce Sales Surged during the Pandemic," Mayumi Brewster, US Census Bureau, April 27, 2022, https://www.census.gov/library/stories/2022/04/ecommerce-sales-surged-during-pandemic.html

14 "E-Commerce Sales Surged during the Pandemic," Brewster

15 "E-Commerce Sales Surged during the Pandemic," Brewster

16 "E-Commerce Sales Surged during the Pandemic," Brewster

17 "State Government Tax Collections Dropped in Second Quarter of 2020," USA Facts, https://usafacts.org/articles/state-tax-revenue-q2-2020-income-sales-covid-budget-qtax

of almost 6 million, and the agency telephone volume nearly quintupled to 195 million calls.[18] The financial situation for so many Americans was dire, and there were certain locations that could reasonably serve as markers for impact elsewhere across the United States. One helpful analysis was conducted by the JPMorgan Chase Institute. The data science team there is first-rate, led by President Chris Wheat. Using a subset of credit card transaction data, they examined trends in local economic activity across sixteen different cities—focusing on typical goods and services such as gas and transportation, groceries, and restaurant spending, as well as payments tied to pharmacies and other consumer services.[19]

Not surprisingly, in the context of business closures and social distancing in the selected cities, the JPMorgan team found that local economic activity in March 2020 declined year over year at an overall rate of approximately 13 percent, with more concentrated drops in low-income neighborhoods.[20] The data also revealed something very interesting. It showed that cities that demonstrated high rates of the COVID-19 virus (e.g., Chicago, Detroit, and New York) did not experience the same retraction as San Francisco, for example, which had a lockdown order in effect in March.[21] This led the researchers to question whether customer sentiment and policy interventions were more responsible for financial outcomes than the actual rate of infection itself.[22]

---

18 *Tax Filing: 2021 Performance Underscores Need for IRS to Address Persistent Challenges*, US Government Accountability Office report, April 2022, https://www.gao.gov/products/gao-22-104938

19 "The Early Impact of COVID-19 on Local Commerce: Changes in Spending Across Neighborhoods and Online," JPMorgan Chase Institute, June 2020, https://www.jpmorganchase.com/institute/all-topics/community-development/report-early-impact-covid-19-local-commerce

20 "The Early Impact of COVID-19 on Local Commerce," JPMorgan Chase Institute

21 "The Early Impact of COVID-19 on Local Commerce," JPMorgan Chase Institute

22 "The Early Impact of COVID-19 on Local Commerce," JPMorgan Chase Institute

And while the public health debate of shutdowns will likely continue for some time, in places like Florida, Governor Ron DeSantis lifted most of the state restrictions by September 2020, allowing for full economic activity and a designation as one of only five states receiving a 100 percent "back-to-normal" rating from Moody's.[23] And the City of Miami enhanced that opportunity even more. As shared by Jennifer Hernandez of the Miami Department of Innovation and Technology, "*When COVID hit, we had to make sure that the Miami community could still access services, and still open businesses. And to keep the economy going, we focused on making sure City services were available digitally—many of which were previously only available in-person.*"[24]

This wave of digitization had massive impacts on the recovery, as convenience and accessibility resulted in efficiencies for residents and commerce—paving the way for relocation of new businesses and access to collaborations across the city.[25] Ms. Hernandez continued, "*Through a partnership with Mastercard, we saw that online spending skyrocketed while in-person spending fell quickly, so we knew that mom-and-pop shops were going to be in trouble. And that helped us improve the services [Miami] provided.*"[26] And this approach did not just help engage with the private sector but also streamlined data sharing to ensure federal dollars and associated opportunities could be enhanced, com-

23 "The Road to Economic Recovery: What Cities Can Teach Us about Managing the COVID-19 Pandemic," Nico Maffey, Data-Smart City Solutions, Harvard University Bloomberg Center for Cities, June 2, 2021, https://datasmart.hks.harvard.edu/news/article/road-economic-recovery-what-cities-can-teach-us-about-managing-covid-19-pandemic

24 "The Road to Economic Recovery: What Cities Can Teach Us," Maffey

25 "The Road to Economic Recovery: What Cities Can Teach Us," Maffey

26 "The Road to Economic Recovery: What Cities Can Teach Us," Maffey (brackets in original)

paring business licensing data with federal resources to better understand which firms were applying for assistance and how to incorporate them into the developing ecosystem model.[27]

With so many communities dependent on sales tax and government fees that are typically paid for in-person business and social activities, the COVID-19 pandemic gutted municipal coffers. Limited consumer spending, construction permit applications, recreational charges, and tourism revenue not only forced a cut in services, but that impact combined with less need also led to furloughs across municipal employees.[28] For example, Cincinnati, Ohio, was forced to lay off fifteen hundred metropolitan employees, while areas such as Richardson, Texas, had a massive shortfall that forced the closure of the town's recreation center.[29] However, some communities sought to address these challenges in different ways. For example, Rochester, New York, allowed its residents significant deferrals of certain property tax and utility payments.[30] Across the country, due to the impacts of the COVID-19 pandemic, it is estimated that nearly nine hundred thousand state, local, and government jobs were cut, forcing all state and local budget directors to navigate a reopened environment while still establishing protocols to creatively manage their workforce and community services in the event of any future pandemic.[31]

While practical research continues to develop at universities and think tanks on the importance of a robust local model to support the small business and workforce ecosystems during a

27 "The Road to Economic Recovery: What Cities Can Teach Us," Maffey

28 *What COVID-19 Means for City Finances*, National League of Cities report

29 *What COVID-19 Means for City Finances*, National League of Cities report

30 *What COVID-19 Means for City Finances*, National League of Cities report

31 *What COVID-19 Means for City Finances*, National League of Cities report

pandemic, among the trials and successes that local economies experienced in 2020 and beyond, there are certainly ideas worth highlighting for future consideration. Whether it is autonomous cars, delivery drones, or something more mainstream, such as self-checkout at the grocery store, urban cities and rural towns will have to incorporate these economic realities into their resilience strategy.[32] But how should we handle some of the in-person components that may very well be required to be addressed? One such area that could be mined by policymakers is a work practice that became commonplace during the pandemic: working from home. While this trend abated markedly after the crisis had passed, much of corporate America has developed a modified strategy that accounts for some flexibility for in-office mandates.

For scale purposes, in 2021, nearly twenty-eight million Americans worked from home—tripling that number from just two years before. This led to companies decreasing real estate space, which resulted in lower property tax revenues and commuting fee income for local economies.[33] In a January 2023 study by JPMorgan Chase, researchers found several interesting impacts of this work-from-home phenomenon. These included the fact that retail growth had followed workers back to suburban communities versus downtown business districts, urban and suburban land use policies had allowed for more hybrid work/living and retail flexibility as part of the development planning, there was potential for

32 *Future of Cities: Reenvisioning Retail for Recovery and Resilience*, National League of Cities report, June 2021, https://www.nlc.org/resource/future-of-cities-reenvisioning-retail-for-recovery-and-resilience/

33 "Downtown Downturn: The COVID-19 Shock to Brick-and-Mortar Retail," JPMorgan Chase Institute, January 2023, https://www.jpmorganchase.com/institute/research/cities-local-communities/downtown-downturn-COVID-19-shock-to-brick-and-mortar

increased taxes to follow the trends into these growing communities to meet greater needs, and meaningful transportation changes could account for variations in ridership.[34]

So, does this mean all of America is moving to the suburbs? Of course not. But it does demonstrate that over time, there is community adaptation to a changing reality. In fact, another work practice, commonly referred to as "short-term work," was used in other parts of the world and proved successful in managing their unemployment rates. Much of Europe utilized short-term work programs in their efforts to address unemployment concerns during the COVID-19 pandemic, ensuring that the growing and healthier sectors of the economy were prioritized over those that were shrinking.[35] By intentionally reducing hours worked by employees, the local municipalities could support changing needs in the economy, thereby increasing production capacity, and, as needed, could sustain employee relationships with employers.[36] The limited hours were complemented by government wage subsidies lasting up to a year, most often paid directly to employees.[37] The results of this program across Europe were successful in that employees only lost about 5 percent of working hours from before the COVID-19 pandemic, and countries such as France and Germany maintained relatively consistent rates of single-digit unemployment from February into April 2020, as

34 "Downtown Downturn: The COVID-19 Shock to Brick-and-Mortar Retail," JPMorgan Chase Institute

35 "Contrasting U.S. and European Job Markets during COVID-19," Jean-Benoît Eyméoud, Nicolas Petrosky-Nadeau, Raül Santaeulàlia-Llopis, and Etienne Wasmer, Federal Reserve Bank of San Francisco, February 22, 2021, https://www.frbsf.org/research-and-insights/publications/economic-letter/2021/02/contrasting-us-and-european-job-markets-during-COVID-19/

36 "Contrasting U.S. and European Job Markets," Eyméoud et al.

37 "Contrasting U.S. and European Job Markets," Eyméoud et al.

opposed to the US, which climbed from historic lows to double digits in early 2020.[38] About half of US states have components of this program, and given the fact that a March 2022 US small business survey by the US Chamber of Commerce demonstrated that almost 40 percent of US small businesses were poised to offer more flexible working hours in the near future, an examination of this framework may be worthwhile.[39]

Another approach that states may want to investigate may already be up and running in certain areas. Some states have developed the concept of infrastructure banks to help develop their local communities. The seed capital for such a project would typically originate with existing government funding, coupled with private sector funds to leverage capabilities to fund municipal projects. This approach has been utilized to establish more robust public-private partnerships to potentially accelerate critical infrastructure needs, giving the state the ability to negotiate advantageous deals that can provide flexibility for private sector consortiums. This has led to the development of and commitments for roads, airports, and advancements in energy grids, the proceeds of which allow states to repurpose funds toward additional infrastructure priorities.[40]

These banks can also establish a revolving loan fund with direct impact on economic development, and in a future crisis,

---

38 "Contrasting U.S. and European Job Markets," Eyméoud et al.

39 "Report Finds Small Businesses Offering More Flexibility, Higher Wages, New Benefits to Find and Keep Workers," Thaddeus Swanek, US Chamber of Commerce, March 29, 2022, https://www.uschamber.com/small-business/report-finds-small-businesses-offering-more-flexibility-higher-wages-new-benefits-to-find-and-keep-workers

40 "State Resource Center: Offering More Flexibility Funding, Financing, and Delivery," National Governors Association, January 29, 2024, https://www.nga.org/projects/state-resource-center-on-innovative-infrastructure-strategies/

they arguably could become a source for block grant funding that is particular to the economic and geographic needs of that state, those counties, and the critical businesses throughout. Such an approach through a capable financial institution committed to a particular region could potentially establish a variety of financial support products responsive to and designed directly for the businesses within their local geographic footprint to assist in the rescue and recovery of local small businesses. If run in a market-based and transparent manner with substantial private sector partnership and expertise, it could potentially serve as a force multiplier for impacted firms and their employees during pandemic times.

Every state, territory, county, city, and town faced a common enemy in the COVID-19 virus, but the battles were somewhat individual, based largely on the spread of the disease, the decisions of local political leaders, and the economic and commercial impacts on the distinct community. While it is nearly impossible to present a defined plan that can be applied everywhere, by studying best practices and components of approaches that worked throughout the country, local leaders can design robust ecosystems and action plans that can be tested so they can be serviceable in times of crises. But this is not as easy as flicking a switch and achieving seamless business continuity. Rather, it takes experimentation and trial and error. However, the true error would be in not having engaged in this experimentation before it is critically necessary. Dr. Osler was a student of Greek science, and it was his position that much of the world was simply based on the accurate observation of nature. However, he also believed that it was the role of modern science to complement this discipline by *interrogating nature* through experimentation.[41] In order for our localities to have a robust blueprint for a future crisis, that ideation and experimentation must begin now.

41 "Dr. William Osler: Some Reflections," Tom Middlebro, *Studies in Canadian Literature*, vol. 5, no. 2, Fall 1980, https://journals.lib.unb.ca/index.php/scl/article/view/7947/9004

CHAPTER SIX

Pandemic Fraud, Abuse, and Risk Frameworks

Get the patient in a good light. Use your five senses. We miss more by not seeing than we do by not knowing.

As mentioned at the close of the last chapter, Dr. Osler's practice of medicine was immersed in the Greek naturalist tradition of science, which focused on careful observation and the rational analysis of those observations.[1] He said, "*The whole art of medicine is in observation...but to educate the eye to see, the ear to hear and the finger to feel takes time, and to make a beginning, to start [students] on the right path is all that we can do...give them good methods and a proper point of view, and all other things will be added as [their] experience.*"[2]

In the field of medicine, observation typically begins with the physical examination, but as Osler scholar Dr. VanderVeer

1 *Osler for White Coat Pockets, A Vade Mecum for Medical Students and Residents*, Joseph B. VanderVeer, MD, and Charles Bryan, MD, American Osler Society (Masthof Press, 2017)

2 *Osler for White Coat Pockets*, VanderVeer and Bryan (brackets in original)

wrote, for many patients, given the various tests and scans available, the traditional annual physical exam has been described as something of a nuisance.[3] It can be costly, time-consuming, and perhaps it doesn't even result in any actionable diagnosis on its own. But the good doctor disagrees with that position, in that a physical examination allows the physician to assess the patient in the context of his or her past and their ever-changing life circumstances.[4] Dr. VanderVeer believes that a physical exam can be of more value than even an X-ray, noting numerous examples of how exams that he has conducted have revealed ailments not caught by the radiographic film.[5] He summed up his position on this topic with the inspiration he received as a young medical student from a sign that hung in the radiology department of his university, which read: "*We see what we look for, we recognize what we know*."[6] This phrase is undoubtedly applicable to the loan audit efforts that have been conducted on the PPP. While the goal of the program was to get money out the door and help support the economy by keeping people employed, on its face it was certainly successful; however, it is important to look beyond that ambitious goal for a closer independent examination, the results of which will provide critical lessons for the future.

While the PPP was comprised of thousands of person-hours of legislative negotiation, rule writing, guidance drafting, and operational acumen, to date the current fraud estimates are somewhere between $36 billion and $200 billion actively stolen

3 *Osler for White Coat Pockets*, VanderVeer and Bryan
4 *Osler for White Coat Pockets*, VanderVeer and Bryan
5 *Osler for White Coat Pockets*, VanderVeer and Bryan
6 *Osler for White Coat Pockets*, VanderVeer and Bryan

from the government.[7] The disparity in amounts is based on the assessment of the Biden administration's SBA leadership versus the SBA Office of the Inspector General (OIG), respectively. The agency has made the case that the OIG has not necessarily distinguished between "potential fraud" and "likely fraud," and commentators have cited that some allegations may ultimately be attributable to technical compliance errors.[8] A better understanding of the final tally may all come out in time, but amidst legislative and administrative changes to the program into the Biden administration, the SBA's independent auditor KPMG cited that the agency management in place in fiscal year 2022 did not maintain adequate controls or oversight of the program.[9]

---

7 "SBA Potentially Lost $200 Billion in Covid Pandemic Relief to Fraud and Abuse, Government Watchdog Finds," Ana Faguy, *Forbes*, June 27, 2023, https://www.forbes.com/sites/anafaguy/2023/06/27/sba-lost-200-billion-in-covid-pandemic-relief-to-fraud-and-abuse-government-watchdog-finds

8 In the SBA's June 21, 2023 memo titled "Response to COVID-19 Pandemic EIDL and PPP Loan Fraud Landscape (Project 23010)," the agency stated that the Office of the Inspector General's report "*presents a summary of loans that are potential fraud as if they were loans that are likely fraud. The white paper provides an estimate of 'potential fraud,' but does not explicitly define the term except mentioning that OIG believes all loans identified 'warrant investigation.*" https://www.sba.gov/sites/default/files/2023-06/SBA%20OIG%20Report%2023-09.pdf. Further, some have identified that technical errors may impact the final determination, stating "*ineligible loans were the result of conduct running the gamut from outright fraud — such as creating sham companies and falsifying employment records to support fraudulent loan applications — to inaccurate certifications of compliance with loan requirements that were often the subject of ambiguous rules.*" "PPP Loan Prosecutions Appear to Be In the Technical Non-Compliance Phase," Arnall Golden Gregory LLP, JD Supra, May 22, 2024, https://www.jdsupra.com/legalnews/ppp-loan-prosecutions-appear-to-be-in-5915564/

9 According to the SBA's independent auditor KPMG's FY 2022 report, "*Management did not adequately design and implement controls to ensure PPP loan guarantees were completely and accurately reviewed to address their respective eligibility flags and ultimately determine their eligibility for forgiveness. Specifically, management did not demonstrate controls over the review and validation of identified flags from the case management system. Additionally, management did not demonstrate effective monitoring controls over the results from the key*

For purposes of background, in its more traditional loan programs, the SBA maintains what is referred to as an enterprise risk management function. This process is based on industry models and has also been honed by the various types of frauds the SBA has encountered over its seventy-year history. Often, new types of frauds are identified in general banking trends or are highlighted by the SBA OIG as part of its mandate to conduct examinations and inspections of agency activities as it implements various methods to prevent fraud and streamline efficiencies to meet the statutory goals of the agency.

While the SBA OIG puts out many reports on a variety of SBA agency activities over the course of the year, the most important of its findings are addressed in the annual assessment of the agency referred to as the "report on management challenges." This report highlights not only the most critical deficiencies that the agency faces over the course of a particular year, but also the improvements that have been made and the work that remains to be completed by the agency to bring a particular issue under control. But of course, this work is not done in a vacuum. The report comes out after much interaction between the SBA OIG and the SBA agency officials to ensure accuracy, clarity, and transparency around the topics highlighted. As one might imagine, most of these do not come as a surprise to the agency officials, as they are a culmination of many of the other one-off issue audits that the SBA OIG has undertaken during the previous months.

---

contractor involved in the review process. The loan guarantees determined by the contractor as 'No Further Action' were not subsequently reviewed by SBA. During fiscal year 2022, $167 billion of loan forgiveness payments were processed for loans determined by the contractor as 'No Further Action.'" https://www.sba.gov/sites/default/files/2022-11/SBA%20OIG%20Report%2023-02.pdf

Before examining the risk management framework particular to the COVID-19 pandemic, we should set a baseline by examining what the SBA's standard risk management process was for its loan programs at the time. Generally speaking, the SBA does not necessarily utilize a one-size-fits-all approach to its risk management practices for its lenders, with particular focus on its flagship 7(a) lending program.[10] This examination process is overseen by the SBA's Office of Credit Risk Management (OCRM), which typically incorporates a framework into its evaluation efforts known as the "PARRiS Risk Measurement Methodology." PARRiS is an acronym standing for:

- ***P*** – Portfolio Performance: Degree of financial risk to SBA that a Lender presents considering overall portfolio performance indicators and attributes.
- ***A*** – Asset Management: Quality of the origination, servicing, and liquidation practices in the Lender's SBA operation.
- ***R*** – Regulatory Compliance: Lender's compliance with SBA Loan Program Requirements.
- ***Ri*** – Risk Management: Overall institution risk and a Lender's use of an effective governance model to identify, understand, and mitigate risk exposure in its 7(a) portfolio.
- ***S*** – Special Items: Additional key metrics or items that are not included in the other components but

10 "Small Business Administration Lending: Risk Management Principles," attachment to OCC Bulletin 2021-34, Office of the Comptroller of the Currency, US Department of the Treasury, August 2021, https://www.occ.gov/news-issuances/bulletins/2021/bulletin-2021-34a.pdf

> may pose risk to SBA or present program integrity concerns.[11]

This is, of course, the broad strokes of the risk management framework, and the individual analysis of each lender is assessed by various qualitative and quantitative factors, some of which are intended to provide various forms of flags to highlight areas that may require additional review. A score associated with the PARRiS Methodology provides part of the necessary feedback to the regulatory staff to account for the safety and soundness of that SBA lender.[12] So, just imagine a risk methodology that has been in place and developed over years and years, and then, almost overnight, there is an entirely new loan product with an eventual price tag of $800 billion that requires some version of an application of this tool.

In 2015, the US Government Accountability Office (GAO), an independent oversight organization within the federal government often referred to as the "congressional watchdog," published a government-wide guidance document titled *A Framework for Managing Fraud Risks in Federal Programs*.[13] The suggested

---

11 "Revised Risk-Based Review/Examination Protocol for SBA Supervised Lenders," US Small Business Administration policy notice, January 18, 2017, https://www.SBA.gov/document/policy-notice-5000-1940-revised-risk-based-reviewexamination-protocol-SBA-supervised-lenders; "Small Business Administration Lending: Risk Management Principles," US Department of the Treasury

12 "Revised Risk-Based Review/Examination Protocol, US Small Business Administration policy notice; "Small Business Administration Lending: Risk Management Principles," Office of the Comptroller of the Currency bulletin attachment

13 *A Framework for Managing Fraud Risks in Federal Programs*, US Government Accountability Office report, July 28, 2015, https://www.gao.gov/products/gao-15-593sp

approach set forth by the GAO was a relatively standard risk management process that sought to inform government management on how a strategic risk assessment approach can be achieved internally in order to avoid or mitigate existing and potential risks through a series of controls serving to advance the agency mission and minimize losses of taxpayer dollars. While the GAO program is general in nature, in order to allow the agency execution teams to include their subject matter expertise in the practical review, it includes the following general principles.[14] First and foremost, it sets forth a commitment to combat fraud with a culture that embraces risk management, citing the need for senior agency leadership to commit to and communicate that same sentiment throughout the entire organization and setting forth defined responsibilities to implement the actions.[15] That responsibility is represented in a process by which the risks are identified, monitored, and assessed to account for changing circumstances, personnel, and additional controls as needed.[16]

Next, the GAO explains that this fraud management program must involve all the relevant stakeholders and determine the likelihood of a particular risk and the risk tolerance that the organization is willing to accept.[17] Once that is in place, the organization must ensure that the control environment is clear, thorough, and comprehensive, so that all parties understand what must be

14 *A Framework for Managing Fraud Risks*, US Government Accountability Office report

15 *A Framework for Managing Fraud Risks*, US Government Accountability Office report

16 *A Framework for Managing Fraud Risks*, US Government Accountability Office report

17 *A Framework for Managing Fraud Risks*, US Government Accountability Office report

done and who is responsible for such actions.[18] All of this information, including the risks, controls, and responsibilities, must be documented so that the entire organization is working collaboratively and not in silos.[19] Upon implementation, risks must be periodically evaluated in a timely fashion to improve processes and identify any additional controls to limit risk to the agency and its operations.[20] This process allows for any further investigation into a risk, so it can be detected and responded to in order to prevent a future occurrence. In this phase, the organization's ability to adapt to changing circumstances is critical, whether it be something as simple as directional signage or as complex as a global pandemic.[21]

So, what was done during PPP and how was this massive program evaluated? Former GAO Director William Shear oversaw an assessment of the operational processes that were in place at the SBA at the time of the implementation of the PPP and how those same procedures accounted for and effectively monitored any associated program risks.[22] The GAO found that in 2020, SBA had established a risk management process to oversee the integrity of the PPP loans, as well as those made as part of the

18 *A Framework for Managing Fraud Risks*, US Government Accountability Office report

19 *A Framework for Managing Fraud Risks*, US Government Accountability Office report

20 *A Framework for Managing Fraud Risks*, US Government Accountability Office report

21 *A Framework for Managing Fraud Risks*, US Government Accountability Office report

22 "COVID-19 Loans: SBA Has Begun to Take Steps to Improve Oversight and Fraud Risk Management," statement of William B. Shear, Director, Financial Markets and Community Investment, US Government Accountability Office, before the House Committee on Small Business, April 20, 2021, https://www.gao.gov/assets/gao-21-498t.pdf

EIDL grant initiative.[23] The GAO reported that the process that SBA engaged in to conduct these reviews included an industry standard sample size of loans for quality control. These loans then underwent review by an automated tool that sought to uncover possible anomalies, noncompliance, and fraud. If flagged for further review, the agency and hired contractors conducted manual reviews, including those which approached the $2 million figure.[24] And as the GAO points out, though, even during these reviews, "*SBA was approving more than 96 percent of the applications within 48 hours after submission.*"[25]

While acknowledging the difficulty of designing, implementing, and delivering such a vast program on an expedited timeline in the midst of emergency circumstances, the GAO did recommend several enhancements to the SBA's loan-making processes under these programs.[26] Noting that the SBA staff did utilize informal methods of fraud risk assessment, including the engagement of subject matter experts for frontline internal control systems, the agency watchdog stressed the need for a more robust formal fraud risk assessment, the development of better data tracking mechanisms, and a more dynamic reporting of improper payments in order to determine the potential size of the fraud pool.[27]

The GAO also zeroed in on particular areas of concern around the PPP loan-making process that focused mostly on the standards that were in place for borrower documentation, the

23 "COVID-19 Loans: SBA Has Begun to Take Steps to Improve Oversight," Shear

24 "COVID-19 Loans: SBA Has Begun to Take Steps to Improve Oversight," Shear

25 "COVID-19 Loans: SBA Has Begun to Take Steps to Improve Oversight," Shear

26 *"While some level of risk may be acceptable in an emergency, an effective internal control system improves accountability and transparency."* (From "COVID-19 Loans: SBA Has Begun to Take Steps to Improve Oversight, Shear.)

27 "COVID-19 Loans: SBA Has Begun to Take Steps to Improve Oversight," Shear

eligibility of those borrowers, and the manner in which those borrowers explained and/or documented the use of the loan proceeds in question.[28] One particular concern raised was the process for borrower self-certifications that they believed made the program particularly vulnerable to fraud, citing the fact that borrowers could ultimately apply for up to $2 million, which established a fertile ground for criminal elements to flourish.[29] GAO noted that the approach that was taken increased program susceptibility to improper payments, particularly in the midst of lenders filing more than twenty-one thousand suspicious activity reports—which are required to be filed by financial institutions under concerning circumstances, such as possible identify theft, use of a dormant businesses, falsified tax documents, forgeries, or rapid movement of funds.[30]

The assessment by the GAO contributed to the significant investigative and prosecutorial activity by the SBA OIG and the Department of Justice. By February 2021, there were over one hundred PPP fraud cases charged, with thirty defendants pleading guilty by that time.[31] But these were just the public cases, as the SBA OIG hotline continued to receive over seventy thousand tips and complaints—which in a typical SBA year would have been closer to seven hundred. As of June 2023, the SBA OIG cited the potential for significant fraud in both the PPP and EIDL programs, and hundreds of individuals have been convicted of criminal charges—with many more cases pending.[32] Some of these

28 "COVID-19 Loans: SBA Has Begun to Take Steps to Improve Oversight," Shear
29 "COVID-19 Loans: SBA Has Begun to Take Steps to Improve Oversight," Shear
30 "COVID-19 Loans: SBA Has Begun to Take Steps to Improve Oversight," Shear
31 "COVID-19 Loans: SBA Has Begun to Take Steps to Improve Oversight," Shear
32 "COVID-19 Loans: SBA Has Begun to Take Steps to Improve Oversight," Shear

statistics were ultimately linked to "*1,050 indictments, 827 arrests, 553 convictions*" and the return of "*over $8 billion in EIDL funds… by financial institutions and another $20 billion by borrowers.*"[33]

Over the course of its work to date, the SBA OIG has provided key recommendations to the agency to reinforce internal controls, including strengthening validation of loan amounts, reviewing employee disbursements and legitimacy of businesses, fortifying US government payment methods within the Department of the Treasury, ensuring loan payments are not made to amended account numbers, revising processes to account for necessary borrower information, monitoring erroneous duplication of payments, and a more robust use of link analysis to potentially highlight "*fraud clusters through shared data attributes.*"[34] The SBA OIG identified several fraud indicators that, when taken together, are tantamount to a "*fingerprint left behind at a crime scene.*"[35] Those include assessments of accounts that demonstrate the following: hold codes flagged for fraud; geolocation analysis for internet protocol addresses associated with borrower applications; duplication of employer identification numbers; changes in deposit accounts of borrowers; nonpayment/default or lack of application for loan forgiveness; affiliated hotline complaints; and/or suspicious physical and email addresses.[36]

---

33 Testimony of Hannibal "Mike" Ware, Inspector General, US Small Business Administration, before the US House Committee on Small Business, July 13, 2023, https://www.SBA.gov/sites/default/files/2023-07/Statement%20for%20the%20Record%2007-13-2023%20FINAL.pdf

34 Testimony of Hannibal "Mike" Ware before the US House Committee on Small Business

35 Testimony of Hannibal "Mike" Ware before the US House Committee on Small Business

36 Testimony of Hannibal "Mike" Ware before the US House Committee on Small Business

With all of this in mind, as of June 2023, the SBA OIG had received 250,000 complaints with nearly 100,000 actionable leads, which that office has estimated "*represent[s] more than 100 years of investigative case work.*"[37] Among other regional investigative initiatives, this work has been supported across multiple government agencies in a task force referred to as the Pandemic Response Accountability Committee (PRAC). These efforts have been both domestic and international in nature, with cross-border cooperation from law enforcement agencies around the world.[38] Some of the more egregious examples on the domestic front outlined by SBA Inspector General Hannibal "Mike" Ware included a regional bank manager in Florida who engaged in a conspiracy to defraud the program of $25 million; a California man who was convicted of defrauding the program by submitting false information to three banks and using funds for personal costs such as luxury vehicles and was sentenced to four-and-half years in prison for what amounted to a $5 million fraud; and a California woman who fled to Montenegro to avoid prison for her thirteen-person conspiracy to defraud the program through a series of synthetic identities of the elderly, deceased, and foreign exchange students, with funds going toward "*gold coins, diamonds, jewelry, luxury watches, designer handbags, cryptocurrency, securities, and a Harley-Davidson motorcycle.*"[39]

In April 2024, the Department of Justice's COVID-19 Fraud Enforcement Task Force, a cross-agency committee of twenty

37 Testimony of Hannibal "Mike" Ware before the US House Committee on Small Business

38 Testimony of Hannibal "Mike" Ware before the US House Committee on Small Business

39 Testimony of Hannibal "Mike" Ware before the US House Committee on Small Business

federal inspectors, announced the seizure of almost $1.5 billion of fraudulently obtained funds and filed charges against approximately 3,500 individuals, with more than half of them already pleading guilty, alongside several hundred civil settlements.[40] These include individuals and rings of fraudulent actors from coast to coast. With the potential for billions of dollars in fraud as identified by the SBA OIG, and GAO estimates of up to $135 billion in unemployment insurance fraud, there has been bipartisan support for increases in the statute of limitations associated with prosecutions in this space in order to recapture as much money as possible from any illicit activities and to ensure that justice is served against all of those responsible.[41] Those will, of course, be decisions that the appropriate authorities will make based on the evidence available to them and the perceived purpose of the identified parties—meaning whether the fraud was intentional, potentially legal but still suspicious, or ultimately deemed a misunderstanding of the program. While the dollar-figure threshold for loan investigations has been something of a moving target, given the back-and-forth between Congress, it appears that the current intention is to recover every cent possible through the agency's own work, as well as the investigative and prosecutorial horsepower of the SBA OIG, PRAC, and the DOJ COVID-19 task force.[42]

To find the fraud around PPP, the government audit and enforcement staff have to truly dig into the loan documents and

40 "Feds Have Seized More than $1.4 Billion from Fraudulent COVID-19 Relief Recipients," James Farrell, *Forbes*, April 9, 2024, https://www.forbes.com/sites/jamesfarrell/2024/04/09/feds-have-seized-more-than-14-billion-from-fraudulent-covid-relief-recipients/

41 "Feds Have Seized More than $1.4 Billion," Farrell

42 "Federal Officials Fear U.S. Won't Pursue Some with Overdue COVID-19 Loans," Tony Room, *Washington Post*, April 3, 2023, https://www.washingtonpost.com/business/2023/04/03/eidl-loans-sba-repayment/

assess trends and crimes that may not be readily apparent at first glance. The importance of this kind of observation is a critical lesson for any professional practice that examines cause and effect. Whether it be medicine, or even loan-making, the keen eye that accounts for public trends, personal histories, and examination details can prove fruitful before, during, and after any diagnosis. During his time as a leader in the field of medicine, Dr. Osler was very open to both traditional and nontraditional methods of treatment, particularly for ailments where current medicine had produced limited success; and he espoused that no physician should be so brazen as to believe that he or she knew all of the answers.[43] Not unlike the PPP—while the science of risk management was available, the program itself was novel, and now that we know where particular risk controls and audit capabilities have proven most effective, we must ensure that any future programs are treated with a very heavy dose of these preventive measures to account for the fraudulent elements of our society. Between this time and the next, new and creative approaches and technologies for both capital distribution and risk controls may very well be readily available, and policymakers must be very open to examining the frameworks that will maximize policy goals while accounting for their role as taxpayer fiduciaries.[44] As has been said of Dr. Osler, "*Although he would fight vigorously to protect the public against frauds and charlatans, he would encourage critical study of whatever therapeutic approaches were reliably reported to be beneficial to patients.*"[45]

---

43 "Healing and Heroism," H. Brownell Wheeler, MD, *New England Journal of Medicine*, vol. 322, no. 21, May 24, 1990, https://www.nejm.org/doi/full/10.1056/NEJM199005243222129

44 "Healing and Heroism," Wheeler

45 "Healing and Heroism," Wheeler

SECTION III

The Lessons for Future Policy Clinicians

CHAPTER SEVEN

Assessment of Global Economic Support for Small and Medium-Sized Businesses

There must be no discrimination by the loyal student, who should willingly draw from any and every source with an open mind and stern resolve to render unto all their dues.

As previously referenced, the "latchkeyer" access that certain lucky students and residents received from Dr. Osler to freely peruse his personal library would serve as a significant benefit to the service of future patients and global medical advancement. It is without question that both the academic and experiential learning of medical knowledge is cumulative, as it often is in economic discovery. There are, of course, basic tenets that are foundational to all professional assessments, but be it the introduction of a new pathogen, treatment, business innovation, or consumer product, they are seemingly ever present and can sometimes impact humanity in almost unimaginable ways. Dr. Osler's medical library was so very special not just because of its sheer size but also due to the curation of texts from great medical intellectuals around the globe, whose collective insights were quite foundational to his own scholarship. And he knew that a myopic view of one's craft was severely limiting, noting that "*[t]he true student is a citizen of the world, the allegiance of whose soul... is too precious to be restricted to a single country*."[1] And so it is the global economic lessons of the COVID-19 pandemic that we will seek to explore here.

Commentators have identified that the COVID-19 pandemic induced the largest economic recession across the world since World War II, citing it as "*the first instance of negative growth in at least 60 years for these countries [Europe] as a group*."[2] Of course, small businesses across the globe faced similar challenges to those in the United States, including limits on cash reserves, where simulation data demonstrated a nearly 90 percent cash exhaustion within three months for certain European countries.[3] With this in mind, global governments acted quickly to support both their small and medium-sized business communities and their workers, which included access to loans and versions of unemployment insurance, as well as other unique financial support mechanisms. While there were policy ideas shared across impacted governments, the size of the US financial response to the COVID-19 pandemic was nota-

1 *Osler: Inspirations from a Great Physician*, Charles S. Bryan (Oxford University Press, 1997)

2 *Financing SMEs and Entrepreneurs (special edition): The Impact of COVID-19 on SME Financing*, Organisation for Economic Co-Operation and Development report (Paris: OECD Publishing, 2020), https://www.oecd.org/unitedstates/financing-smes-and-entrepreneurship-an-oecd-scoreboard-ecd81a65-en.htm

3 *Financing SMEs and Entrepreneurs 2022: SME Finance in COVID-19 Recovery Packages: Assessment and Implications*, Organisation for Economic Co-Operation and Development report (Paris: OECD Publishing, 2022), https://www.oecd-ilibrary.org/industry-and-services/financing-smes-and-entrepreneurs-2022_44db9703-en

bly larger than anywhere else in the world—more than 50 percent greater than the UK response and three times that of France. New Zealand served as the only country to match the financial appropriations of the US based on size of economy.[4] And in the midst of all of this, global governments were struggling to determine the most viable economic path forward, as demonstrated by former SBA Administrator and Harvard University Fellow Karen Mills who shared that she had been approached by countries such as the UK, Saudi Arabia, and Spain asking *"for the blueprint of the SBA because they want[ed] to copy it."*[5]

Notwithstanding the lending programs that so much of the world utilized early on to support its small business community, as has been alluded to, many countries outside of the US seemingly split their pandemic support into two categories. The first was the "Rescue Period"—perhaps the first four to five months of the COVID-19 pandemic, with the remainder of the time deemed to be something of a "Recovery Period" for these nations. The reason for this was in large part to avoid a liquidity crisis early on, which then allowed a policy pivot to provide foundational support for sustainable resilience and growth.[6] While jurisdictions like Canada embraced a forgivable loan comparable to the US early on, according to data provided by the Organisation for Economic Co-operation and Development (OECD), many countries prioritized more dedicated financial support to the self-em-

4 *Financing SMEs and Entrepreneurs 2022: SME Finance in COVID-19 Recovery Packages*, Organisation for Economic Co-Operation and Development report

5 "Small-Business Owners Say PPP Isn't the Solution They Need," Devin Leonard, Bloomberg, May 7, 2020, https://www.bloomberg.com/news/features/2020-05-07/small-business-owners-say-ppp-isn-t-covid-19-solution-they-need

6 *Financing SMEs and Entrepreneurs 2022: SME Finance in COVID-19 Recovery Packages*, Organisation for Economic Co-Operation and Development report

ployed during the Rescue Period, while growing opportunities for startup businesses went from 2 percent during the Rescue Period to almost 25 percent during the Recovery Period.[7]

As was seen in America, banks around the world were a critical partner in advancing recovery loans to struggling small businesses. This was of particular importance for the countries that did not develop a comparable forgivable loan concept like PPP but rather sought to address traditional loan-making through lower-interest monetary policy.[8] Along with traditional banks, other digital platforms and fintechs were widely used in this effort, with countries like Switzerland and Korea highlighted as having particularly effective channels for distribution.[9] But even in the scenarios where access to loans and equity injections were available, many countries required that recipient businesses demonstrate some level of commercial viability.[10] For example, as of May 2021, Australia required that companies show an actual year-over-year decline to demonstrate that they had been revenue-generating; whereas at approximately the same time, the United Kingdom required a showing of viability and that the business not be in a collective insolvency.[11] Greece also embraced a demonstration of business sustainability in certain circumstances, tying lending to the demonstration a recent merger, acquisition, or a cooper-

7 *Financing SMEs and Entrepreneurs 2022: SME Finance in COVID-19 Recovery Packages*, Organisation for Economic Co-Operation and Development report

8 *Financing SMEs and Entrepreneurs 2022: SME Finance in COVID-19 Recovery Packages*, Organisation for Economic Co-Operation and Development report

9 *Financing SMEs and Entrepreneurs 2022: SME Finance in COVID-19 Recovery Packages*, Organisation for Economic Co-Operation and Development report

10 *Financing SMEs and Entrepreneurs 2022: SME Finance in COVID-19 Recovery Packages*, Organisation for Economic Co-Operation and Development report

11 *Financing SMEs and Entrepreneurs 2022: SME Finance in COVID-19 Recovery Packages*, Organisation for Economic Co-Operation and Development report

ation agreement to advance revenue over the course of the next five years.[12]

But traditional loan programs were, of course, not the only international instrument used. In the United Kingdom for example, the government established "Bounce Back loans," where private lenders were able to not only accept a fully backed government guarantee but also write off the loans as well.[13] In fact, with an economic contraction of nearly 10 percent in 2020, the UK incorporated a number of economic initiatives in its response to the COVID-19 pandemic. It provided direct grants for smaller and impacted firms, as well as subsidized its social safety nets to support sick and other vulnerable populations.[14] Beyond just the Bounce Back loan program, the UK also maintained the Self -Employment Income Support Scheme, where the government covered 80 percent of taxable revenues for the self-employed up to £7,500, which continued throughout the pandemic but was scaled back over the course of the Recovery Period.[15] The country also instituted an unemployment support initiative called the Coronavirus Job Retention Scheme, where furloughed workers were able to access up to £2,500 per month.[16]

Closer to the end of 2020, the UK introduced its Pay As You Grow model, which gave the Bounce Back loan recipients the

12 *Financing SMEs and Entrepreneurs 2022: SME Finance in COVID-19 Recovery Packages*, Organisation for Economic Co-Operation and Development report

13 *Financing SMEs and Entrepreneurs 2022: SME Finance in COVID-19 Recovery Packages*, Organisation for Economic Co-Operation and Development report

14 *Financing SMEs and Entrepreneurs 2022: SME Finance in COVID-19 Recovery Packages*, Organisation for Economic Co-Operation and Development report

15 *Financing SMEs and Entrepreneurs 2022: SME Finance in COVID-19 Recovery Packages*, Organisation for Economic Co-Operation and Development report

16 *Financing SMEs and Entrepreneurs 2022: SME Finance in COVID-19 Recovery Packages*, Organisation for Economic Co-Operation and Development report

ability to make interest-only payments on those loans after a certain period.[17] Impacted business were also given grants of up to £1,500 on nearly a monthly basis, as well as job search support for those on the unemployment assistance program—known as the Job Entry Targeted Support, or JETS, program.[18] In the second and third waves of funding, businesses in the accommodation and leisure industries received additional targeted grant support as well.[19] Alongside a statutory sick pay program to allow for self-isolation under the public health guidance, the UK also embraced programs supporting businesses that hired new apprentices—covering a certain level of wages in support of these workers and businesses.[20] In order to continue commercial innovation, the UK additionally established funding for businesses through its Future Fund loan to enhance the development of certain high-growth companies that had received at least £250,000 in equity investment over the previous three years.[21]

While wide-ranging debt programs to sustain small businesses impacted by the COVID-19 pandemic received generally favorable reviews from their constituencies, monetary policy also played an important role in stemming economic turmoil. For example, the Mexican central bank eventually reduced interest rates to 4.5 percent, and Japan saw large increases in commer-

17 *Financing SMEs and Entrepreneurs 2022: SME Finance in COVID-19 Recovery Packages*, Organisation for Economic Co-Operation and Development report

18 *Financing SMEs and Entrepreneurs 2022: SME Finance in COVID-19 Recovery Packages*, Organisation for Economic Co-Operation and Development report

19 *Financing SMEs and Entrepreneurs 2022: SME Finance in COVID-19 Recovery Packages*, Organisation for Economic Co-Operation and Development report

20 *Financing SMEs and Entrepreneurs 2022: SME Finance in COVID-19 Recovery Packages*, Organisation for Economic Co-Operation and Development report

21 *Financing SMEs and Entrepreneurs 2022: SME Finance in COVID-19 Recovery Packages*, Organisation for Economic Co-Operation and Development report

cial business lending in the first half of 2020 on the back of an attractive interest rate environment.[22] Some countries highlighted the need to include novel insolvency measures in their policies. Examples included the Netherlands offering opportunities for loan restructuring using credit as working capital or business restart funding, Singapore's policies permitting lower creditor approval thresholds in their program, and places like Ireland, Portugal, and Spain streamlining administrative restructuring procedures.[23] In fact, Portuguese leaders went so far as to engage their judiciary to modernize its legal framework for insolvency.[24] And regulatory changes were seen in varying degrees throughout Europe, as efforts to open up research and development patent designs were advanced, along with the European Parliament's 2021 efforts to simplify investor access to small and medium-sized businesses and New Zealand's efforts to reduce disclosure provisions that presented compliance burdens to various small and medium-sized companies.[25]

Interestingly, private investment was a significant focus for several European countries. For example, France implemented a loan and subordinated debt initiative to incentivize private capital, which was distributed by banks.[26] This fund held up to a 30 percent government-backed guarantee with a fixed interest rate

---

22 *Financing SMEs and Entrepreneurs 2022: SME Finance in COVID-19 Recovery Packages*, Organisation for Economic Co-Operation and Development report

23 *Financing SMEs and Entrepreneurs 2022: SME Finance in COVID-19 Recovery Packages*, Organisation for Economic Co-Operation and Development report

24 *Financing SMEs and Entrepreneurs 2022: SME Finance in COVID-19 Recovery Packages*, Organisation for Economic Co-Operation and Development report

25 *Financing SMEs and Entrepreneurs 2022: SME Finance in COVID-19 Recovery Packages*, Organisation for Economic Co-Operation and Development report

26 *Financing SMEs and Entrepreneurs 2022: SME Finance in COVID-19 Recovery Packages*, Organisation for Economic Co-Operation and Development report

of up to 6 percent.[27] The New Zealand government followed suit by opening its own fund in 2020 where it put up $150 million alongside an additional $420 million of private capital to support the small and medium-sized business community.[28] In this same vein, the UK incorporated its securities markets into the pandemic response by partnering with key asset managers and the London Stock Exchange to invest funding into both private companies and small public companies positioned for investment.[29]

Alternative finance approaches also played a unique role in various countries around the world. While the list of innovations was long, countries like Australia, Bulgaria, Croatia, France, Ireland, Italy, Lithuania, Malaysia, and Peru all sought to advance various approaches that incorporated real estate and equipment finance leasing, reverse factoring for trade receivables, crowdfunding, private equity advice, network access, export credit advice, and reinsurance options—much of which sought to address liquidity in the tightening international supply chain ecosystem.[30] And among these financial strategies, certain countries sought to strengthen non-financial, educational, and technical assistance support for the impacted businesses. While the US small business community received traditional support from both government and nonprofits like the SBA, Small Business Development Centers (SBDC) network, Women's Business Centers, Veteran Business Outreach

27 *Financing SMEs and Entrepreneurs 2022: SME Finance in COVID-19 Recovery Packages*, Organisation for Economic Co-Operation and Development report

28 *Financing SMEs and Entrepreneurs 2022: SME Finance in COVID-19 Recovery Packages*, Organisation for Economic Co-Operation and Development report

29 *Financing SMEs and Entrepreneurs 2022: SME Finance in COVID-19 Recovery Packages*, Organisation for Economic Co-Operation and Development report

30 *Financing SMEs and Entrepreneurs 2022: SME Finance in COVID-19 Recovery Packages*, Organisation for Economic Co-Operation and Development report

Centers, the Service Corps of Retired Executives (SCORE), and some corporate responsibility efforts from large companies, other countries concentrated on financial health education as a key component of loan repayment approach.[31] For example, Austria, Denmark, and Lithuania set aside tens of millions of dollars for counseling support, while Germany and Spain focused on strengthening digital resources to advance these goals.[32]

In July, European Union leaders developed a resilience fund of about €750 billion to focus on the Recovery Period effort.[33] A significant portion of the fund was focused on jobs, workers, and temporary business support to mitigate unemployment risks and, as discussed earlier, develop short-time work schemes, given the concerns associated with the correlation between labor flexibility and business continuity.[34] Countries like Switzerland embraced short-term work allowances to supplement their self-employed community, a bridge loan initiative, certain social safety net payment deferrals, and extensions for tax and other payments for federal suppliers.[35] The French approach also included several of these components, as well as direct financial support and postponement of rent/utilities for impacted small businesses. Places like Ireland maintained an interest-free lending initiative for small and medium-sized businesses, where eligibility was contingent on sustained

31 *Financing SMEs and Entrepreneurs 2022: SME Finance in COVID-19 Recovery Packages*, Organisation for Economic Co-Operation and Development report

32 *Financing SMEs and Entrepreneurs 2022: SME Finance in COVID-19 Recovery Packages*, Organisation for Economic Co-Operation and Development report

33 *Financing SMEs and Entrepreneurs 2022: SME Finance in COVID-19 Recovery Packages*, Organisation for Economic Co-Operation and Development report

34 *Financing SMEs and Entrepreneurs 2022: SME Finance in COVID-19 Recovery Packages*, Organisation for Economic Co-Operation and Development report

35 *Financing SMEs and Entrepreneurs 2022: SME Finance in COVID-19 Recovery Packages*, Organisation for Economic Co-Operation and Development report

revenue decreases.[36] By comparison, in Japan's special credit guarantee program, the country relied on approaches utilized in earlier banking crises where certain loans were conditioned on typically negative criteria, such as tax delinquencies or previous loan default, although this program did exhibit misuse and fraud.[37]

Targeted business and employee support systems were easier in certain countries because administrative systems for monitoring employee hours were available to those governments prior to the pandemic. This is an important point to consider in the planning for any future crises, as it allowed many countries to focus on their own particular economic vulnerabilities.[38] Alongside this detail, there were also common industry impacts across many countries around the globe. Take, for example, hotels, which saw limited activity due to fear of contagion and travel, enforcement of home lockdowns, and restricted access to workforce. Marriott International furloughed tens of thousands of its nearly 175,000 employees worldwide, and Hilton Worldwide took on a revolving loan of $1.75 billion as a business precaution early in the pandemic.[39] And of course, the supply chain for food delivery, farmers,

---

36 *Financing SMEs and Entrepreneurs 2022: SME Finance in COVID-19 Recovery Packages*, Organisation for Economic Co-Operation and Development report

37 *Financing SMEs and Entrepreneurs 2022: SME Finance in COVID-19 Recovery Packages*, Organisation for Economic Co-Operation and Development report

38 *Financing SMEs and Entrepreneurs 2022: SME Finance in COVID-19 Recovery Packages*, Organisation for Economic Co-Operation and Development report; "The $800 Billion Paycheck Protection Program: Where Did the Money Go and Why Did It Go There?" David Autor, David Cho, Leland D. Crane, Mita Goldar, Byron Lutz, Joshua Montes, William B. Peterman, David Ratner, Daniel Villar, and Ahu Yildirmaz, National Bureau of Economic Research, January 2022, https://www.nber.org/system/files/working_papers/w29669/w29669.pdf

39 "COVID-19 Outbreak: Impact on Global Economy," Saira Naseer, Sidra Khalid, Summaria Parveen, Kashif Abbass, Huaming Song, and Monica Violeta Achim, *Frontiers in Public Health*, January 30, 2023; available at NIH National Library of Medicine: https://www.ncbi.nlm.nih.gov/pmc/articles/PMC9923118/

purveyors, processors, and the like all underwent substantial challenges, which led to significant food storages in many households in various countries. In the UK, for example, the nearly £1 billion worth of rations being stored in homes had a downstream impact on food distribution, access, and the operational capabilities of community food banks at a time when this access was desperately needed.[40] And of course, due to the virus, most community events—large and small—were scratched. The British Open was canceled. The Tokyo Olympics were postponed. And the lack of recreational attendance at the movies led the film industry's revenue to fall by almost 85 percent, resulting in losses of billions of dollars worldwide.[41]

Some have argued that a global action plan to coordinate country policies—particularly as they impact globally aligned industries—may be a wise approach going forward during such emergencies to fend off collective recession tied to these important parts of their economies. For businesses to maximize their capabilities during this time, the environments that the governments create are absolutely critical, and there are many options available to them during both the Rescue and Recovery Periods. Loan programs, direct capital injections, short-term labor, tax deferrals, alternative finance vehicles, public-private partnerships, cost reductions, labor readiness programs, and investments in innovation, among others, are all available tools to be considered when seeking to manage a crisis.[42] Enabling industries and communities to fully embrace their capacities will likely require a

40 "COVID-19 Outbreak: Impact on Global Economy," Naseer et al.

41 "COVID-19 Outbreak: Impact on Global Economy," Naseer et al.

42 *Financing SMEs and Entrepreneurs 2022: SME Finance in COVID-19 Recovery Packages*, Organisation for Economic Co-Operation and Development report

variety of government supports coupled with the removal of both financial and regulatory obstacles to stimulate growth, including the potential incubation of certain local industries and reskilling to encourage local growth and stability.[43] Such best practices could potentially be championed by global organizations, such as the United Nations or the World Bank Group, and perhaps could become even more granular through development banks that focus on a particular region—especially on key topics such as infrastructure and food security.[44]

A journey around the world looking for solutions to this problem is time well spent. As a young physician, Dr. Osler also traveled across North America and Europe to learn at the feet of some of the world's most renowned physicians. In places like Berlin, London, Paris, and Vienna, he found his own calling and recognized how he could contribute to society.[45] He understood that access to different people and different methods would provide a critical, fresh perspective to his work and the work of all professionals trying to advance opportunities for others, noting in full:

> *"The great minds, the great works transcend all limitations of time, of language, and of race.... I care not in what subject he may work, the full knowledge cannot be reached without drawing on the supplies from other lands than his own—French, English, German,*

---

43 "Creating Economic Recovery and Growth After COVID-19," Jessica Shannon and Ingris Carlson, PwC, https://www.pwc.com/gx/en/industries/government-public-services/six-challenges/economic-recovery-after-COVID-19.html

44 "COVID-19 Outbreak: Impact on Global Economy," Naseer et al.

45 *Osler: Inspirations from a Great Physician*, Bryan

> *American, Japanese, Russian, Italian—there must be no discrimination by the loyal student, who should willingly draw from any and every source with an open mind and stern resolve to render unto all their dues.*"[46]

The application of Dr. Osler's approach to international learning is of great value to the work here in that by examining these different approaches, we can compare the data and successes and perhaps duplicate pieces of those policy regimens in the US response to the next pandemic, particularly noting how the implementation of a Rescue Period and Recovery Period for different products and approaches may be of value to the variously sized models of the US small business community.

---

46 *Osler: Inspirations from a Great Physician*, Bryan

CHAPTER EIGHT

The Impacts of Modern Pandemics and Previous US Economic Crises

The person who takes medicine must recover twice, once from the disease and once from the medicine.

THE COVID-19 PANDEMIC HAS IMPACTED global populations in lasting ways. People lost loved ones, and many still maintain long-term health impacts from the infection. Jobs vanished. Businesses closed. And those who survived still face lasting economic hurdles tied to inflation and labor markets, and perhaps even debt associated with non-PPP loans and credit. Everyone did the best they could with the information available to them at the time—citizens and governments alike. Dr. Osler recognized that treatments and medicines were not necessarily cure-alls, in that their mere digestion could lead to tangential challenges and unintended consequences. He said that scientific truth is "*conditioned by the state of knowledge at the time of its announcement.*"[1]

1 *William Osler: A Life in Medicine*, Michael Bliss (University of Toronto Press, 1999)

And that was the essence of PPP in that it made the most sense to achieve the goals of avoiding economic catastrophe at the time. But the hangover of its impact could be with the American taxpayer for generations.

Whether one agrees with the approach of PPP or not, there is no going back, and what we can do now is recognize its successes and challenges and assure the American people that the lessons will be developed and heeded accordingly. For all his achievements and recognitions, Dr. Osler was not always correct. And when he wasn't, such as a time he misdiagnosed a tumor for a distended bladder, he used it as something of a teachable moment to his students to ensure that they knew that failure was part of progress. Of course, the stakes around incorrect or incomplete judgments associated with treating a human life or the economy of an entire nation are of the direst consequences, but not learning from that circumstance would arguably be the biggest failure of all. Dr. Osler believed that physicians should always strive for the best treatments available and continue to learn from the successes and errors of others in order to treat their patients accordingly. In certain pandemic-like viruses, oftentimes the symptoms will present similarly to previously encountered cases, and whether it is an ailing patient or an economic crisis, to borrow a phrase from American author Mark Twain and put it in the context of the COVID-19 virus, "*History may not repeat itself, but it often rhymes.*"

As referenced earlier, the modern pandemic was predated by such well known scourges as the Athenian Plague (430 BC) and the Antonine Plague (AD 165–180).[2] While the prior killed

2 "Pandemics Throughout the History," Shrikanth Sampath, Anwar Khedr, Shahraz Qamar, Aysun Tekin, Romil Singh, Ronya Green, and Rahul Kashyap, monitoring editors: Alexander Muacevic and John R Adler, *Cureus*, vol. 13, no. 9, September 2021; available at NIH National Library of Medicine: https://www.ncbi.nlm.nih.gov/pmc/articles/PMC8525686/

approximately a quarter of the city's population, the latter decimated up to a third of the Roman people, including the Roman leader, Marcus Aurelius.[3] A few hundred years later, in the decade of AD 540, the Justinianic Plague ravaged the Mediterranean region, followed nearly a millennium later by the bubonic plague, which sustained from 346 to 1353. Known as the Black Death, this pandemic may have killed as many as two hundred million people, which was over half of Europe's population at the time.[4] Of note, the Black Death had a curious economic impact, leading to the development of various productivity innovations to account for lost labor, not unlike the modern-day equivalent of work-from-home technologies developed during the COVID-19 pandemic.[5] Several hundred years later, in 1817, the first of the seven cholera pandemics struck parts of Asia and the Middle East—beginning as one waterborne illness, followed closely by another five pandemics from 1827 to 1923, costing over a million lives.[6] The seventh cholera pandemic started in 1961 and continues today.[7]

A review of historic health pandemics of the modern era can serve as a helpful adviser to future events.[8] Notwithstanding the COVID-19 virus's impacts on the coastal parts of the country, disease that reached that level was typically brought in through sailors entering major port cities, with a slow contagion inland; but the advent of modern air travel, international war, and glo-

3 "Pandemics Throughout the History," Sampath et al.

4 "Pandemics Throughout the History," Sampath et al.

5 "Pandemics Throughout the History," Sampath et al.

6 "Pandemics Throughout the History," Sampath et al.

7 "Pandemics Throughout the History," Sampath et al.

8 "Flashback and Lessons Learnt from History of Pandemics before COVID-19, Shivay Parihar, Rimple Jeet Kaur, and Surjit Singh, *Journal of Family Medicine and Primary Care*, vol. 10, no. 7, July 2021, https://journals.lww.com/jfmpc/fulltext/2021/10070/flashback_and_lessons_learnt_from_history_of.3.aspx

balization have dramatically changed the pandemic world.[9] The 1918 Spanish Flu hit the world in various waves and is believed to have started in the US in Kansas via American soldiers' military camps during World War I. This pandemic was one of the first that saw the therapeutic impact of nurses in health care, as there were no antivirals to be provided to those infected or at risk.[10] The medical preventions associated with this plague included social distancing and a curfew, each of which was believed to prevent close contact.[11] Over the course of that epidemic, cities closed restaurants and public gathering places, and ultimately the economy did not fall into a recession.[12] It is believed that over five hundred million people have been infected with this virus, with millions dying, including several hundred thousand in the US alone.[13] In 1957, the H2N2 influenza A virus spread from China to Western Europe and into the United States, claiming as many as a million lives, or more, within the time it was particularly active.[14] A follow-on virus, H3N2, originated ten years later out of Hong Kong and spread globally as soldiers returned home from the Vietnam War, with the disease killing as many as four million people.[15]

---

9 "Fight the Pandemic, Save the Economy: Lessons from the 1918 Flu," Sergio Correia, Stephan Luck, and Emil Verner, *Liberty Street Economics* blog, Federal Reserve Bank of New York, https://libertystreeteconomics.newyorkfed.org/2020/03/fight-the-pandemic-save-the-economy-lessons-from-the-1918-flu/

10 "Pandemics Throughout the History," Sampath et al.

11 "Flashback and Lessons Learnt from History of Pandemics," Parihar, Kaur, and Singh

12 "Flashback and Lessons Learnt from History of Pandemics," Parihar, Kaur, and Singh

13 "Fight the Pandemic, Save the Economy"; "Spanish Flu," Cleveland Clinic, September 21, 2021, https://my.clevelandclinic.org/health/diseases/21777-spanish-flu

14 "Pandemics Throughout the History," Sampath et al.

15 "Pandemics Throughout the History," Sampath et al.

In November 2002, the severe acute respiratory syndrome (SARS) was detected globally, caused by a virus that belongs to the coronavirus family. Originating in China, the death toll remained under one thousand as precautions were implemented including the wearing of masks, handwashing, disinfecting, the closing of entertainment venues and schools, and the timely flow of information for policymaking.[16] This was declared to be over by the summer of 2003.[17] In 2009, the world experienced the swine flu, caused by the H1N1 virus. This episode seems to have started in Mexico and spread to the United States.[18] While the mortality rate was not nearly as severe as the Spanish Flu, for example, perhaps due in part to certain preventive measures, including school closures and various preparedness strategies to support modern medicine, like isolation and contract tracing,[19] it was often referred to as the "*panicdemic*" due to the alarm it caused across international health organizations, spreading to 122 countries in a matter of six weeks.[20] The second wave of this pandemic, Middle East respiratory syndrome coronavirus (MERS-CoV), developed in 2012–2013; however, it was not as severe given that the virus had a low transmissibility.[21] In that time frame, the world was introduced to the Ebola virus epidemic. Mostly geographically limited to the coast of Western Africa, this disease carried fatality rates as high as 70 percent and was particularly

16 "Flashback and Lessons Learnt from History of Pandemics," Parihar, Kaur, and Singh

17 "Pandemics Throughout the History," Sampath et al.

18 "Pandemics Throughout the History," Sampath et al.

19 "Flashback and Lessons Learnt from History of Pandemics," Parihar, Kaur, and Singh

20 "Pandemics Throughout the History," Sampath et al.

21 "Flashback and Lessons Learnt from History of Pandemics," Parihar, Kaur, and Singh

impactful across developing countries, killing over ten thousand people.[22] Methods of contact tracing, quarantine, and the sharing of clinical data were frequently implemented and important for protecting against severe outbreaks.

And while certain public health methodologies have been fashioned and evaluated over the course of these more recent outbreaks, an often overlooked component of pandemics is the impact on mental health. The effects of the COVID-19 virus led to significant global epidemics of loneliness and anxiety, causing a spike in addiction, mental and behavioral health impacts, and suicides. In fact, in March 2022, the World Health Organization reported that during the first year of the COVID-19 pandemic, there was a global increase of 25 percent in anxiety and depression.[23] First responders burned out due to the nonstop and overwhelming pace of caregiving; and the daily reports of cases and death tolls, concerns over economic livelihoods, shortages of available supermarket food items and other supplies, and streams of misinformation all added to the general social concerns.[24] This became so significant throughout the US that President Trump signed an executive order and released an available resources report on the topic in October 2020 entitled *Saving Lives Through Increased Support for Mental and Behavioral Health Needs*, which sought to identify, centralize, and distribute access to the many

22 "Flashback and Lessons Learnt from History of Pandemics," Parihar, Kaur, and Singh

23 "COVID-19 Pandemic Triggers Increase in Prevalence of Anxiety and Depression Worldwide," World Health Organization, March 2, 2022, https://www.who.int/news/item/02-03-2022-covid-19-pandemic-triggers-25-increase-in-prevalence-of-anxiety-and-depression-worldwide#:~:text=In%20the%20first%20year%20of,Health%20Organization%20(WHO)%20today

24 "Pandemics Throughout the History," Sampath et al.

federal government programs that existed and develop local outreach capabilities to combat this scourge.[25]

And while the health implications of these calamities are foundational to this analytical effort, in order to understand historic economic response policies, we should briefly examine some of the more well-known financial crises across modern American history. Perhaps the most notable was the Great Depression, which lasted from 1929 to 1941. It began with a stock market crash and included a series of regional banking panics that led to a technical collapse of the US banking system in 1933.[26] The economic collapse was unprecedented and policymakers at the time did not maintain effective risk mechanisms to avoid such a catastrophe.[27] While certain well-intentioned approaches by the Federal Reserve were deemed to be too little too late, the overall crisis was addressed through sweeping banking reforms and a massive works program as part of President Franklin Roosevelt's New Deal.[28] The economic approach mustered by President Roosevelt was something of a giant laboratory experiment that included components such as cash payments to farmers, debt relief for mortgages, public works projects for the unemployed, and low-interest loans to stricken banks and railroads.[29] And as a result of the Great Depression, the Federal Reserve became a more modern central bank that has proven critical in respond-

---

25 *Saving Lives Through Increased Support for Mental and Behavioral Health Needs*, US Department of Health and Human Services Substance Abuse and Mental Health Services Administration report, December 2020, https://www.samhsa.gov/sites/default/files/saving-lives-mental-behavioral-health-needs.pdf

26 "The Great Depression," Gary Richardson, Federal Reserve History, https://www.federalreservehistory.org/essays/great-depression

27 "The Great Depression," Richardson

28 "The Great Depression," Richardson

29 "The Great Depression," Richardson

ing to more recent financial crises over the years, including the response to the COVID-19 pandemic.[30]

While the country undergoes or scratches the surface of a milder economic recession every so often, there were a couple of historic events that occurred in the early 2000s—which required emergency policy models to help sustain the economy.[31] The first was the September 11, 2001, terrorist attack on the United States. The aerial attacks that imploded the Twin Towers in New York City, leveled part of the US Pentagon, and resulted in the downing of a plane in Pennsylvania cost almost three thousand American souls. It left behind so many grieving families, caused long-standing panic and anxiety across the country, led to a new American war, and devastated the economies of major cities and financial hubs, along with industries such as the airlines, tourism, hospitality, entertainment, and some financial services firms.[32] The Dow Jones Industrial Average lost over 14 percent after the first full week of trading, and the S&P 500 was down nearly 12 percent, with airlines and insurance stocks being the hardest hit.[33]

Ultimately, as part of its response, Congress would pass the Terrorism Risk Insurance Act to ensure that insurance could be reasonably managed so that the government and the insurance industry would share in the massive losses associated with the estimated $40 billion in claims.[34] The discussion of access to legislative

30 "The Great Depression," Richardson

31 "Flashback and Lessons Learnt from History of Pandemics," Parihar, Kaur, and Singh

32 *The Economic Effects of 9/11: A Retrospective Assessment*, Congressional Research Service report, https://www.everycrsreport.com/files/20020927_RL31617_ad8180d7c4ff0117f3d3bd753c398317631b870f.pdf

33 *The Economic Effects of 9/11: A Retrospective Assessment*, Congressional Research Service report

34 *The Economic Effects of 9/11: A Retrospective Assessment*, Congressional Research Service report

action on business interruption insurance was a frequent topic of debate and potential legislation during the COVID-19 pandemic.[35] The idea here is that insurers could be liable for the sustained loss of revenue associated with the business conditions impacted by such an emergency. Such circumstances were not specifically accounted for in most business interruption policies, absent an explicit rider to the contrary. Insurers were, of course, against payments associated with this type of claim that a blanket pandemic scenario could be covered, as forcing the issue could lead to an excessive strain on the insurance industry. That said, even President Trump considered this option at one point, but ultimately, discussions led by Republican senators demonstrated that the avalanche of ex post facto claims would not only rewrite commercially agreed to contracts but could crash the entire insurance system, putting legitimate insurance payments in significant jeopardy.[36]

After September 11, from an international perspective, oil prices spiked briefly and the US experienced some limited trade disruptions.[37] Commentators have assessed that while initial legislative efforts focused on impacted workers, much of the final legislation addressed economy-wide issues.[38] And with the massive financial impact on Manhattan, including an estimated $6.4 billion loss in labor earning and nearly six thousand hotel jobs,

---

35 *Business Interruption Insurance and COVID-19*, Congressional Research Service report, https://crsreports.congress.gov/product/pdf/IN/IN11295

36 Letter from Republican Senators to The Honorable Donald J. Trump, President of the United States of America, April 10, 2020, https://www.scott.senate.gov/wp-content/uploads/imo/media/doc/20.04.10%20Sen.%20Tim%20Scott%20Letter%20on%20BI%20Insurance.pdf

37 *The Economic Effects of 9/11: A Retrospective Assessment*, Congressional Research Service report

38 *The Economic Effects of 9/11: A Retrospective Assessment*, Congressional Research Service report

along with a physical damage cost of well beyond $20 billion, a variety of federal, state, and local economic recovery initiatives went into effect.[39] Alongside so many people losing their lives and their livelihoods, many experienced physical ailments associated with inhalation and an innumerable number of local residents turned to increased use of alcohol and marijuana to deal with depression and bouts of post-traumatic stress disorder.[40]

From a recovery perspective, under the leadership of then President George W. Bush, the disaster function of the federal government support came from the Federal Emergency Management Agency (FEMA), along with disaster loans from the SBA, Department of Labor support for displaced workers, and disaster site funding from the Environmental Protection Agency.[41] President Bush also signed the National Defense Authorization Act for Fiscal Year 2002, providing for substantial block grants of approximately $2 billion in economic recovery support in New York City, which included funding for impacted small businesses throughout the various regions associated with the attacks.[42] On September 23, 2001, President Bush signed Congress's $15 billion Air Transportation Safety and System Stabilization Act, which aided the airline industry through a combination of direct payments and loans.[43]

---

39 *The Economic Effects of 9/11: A Retrospective Assessment*, Congressional Research Service report

40 *The Economic Effects of 9/11: A Retrospective Assessment*, Congressional Research Service report

41 *The Economic Effects of 9/11: A Retrospective Assessment*, Congressional Research Service report

42 *The Economic Effects of 9/11: A Retrospective Assessment*, Congressional Research Service report

43 *The Economic Effects of 9/11: A Retrospective Assessment*, Congressional Research Service report

A noteworthy report was released in July 2004 in response to the September 11 attacks by an independent bipartisan commission created by Congress. The National Commission on Terrorist Attacks Upon the United States, more commonly known as the 9/11 Commission, was charged with conducting a full after-action report of the attacks, including preparedness strategies for future incidents. As part of this strategy, in chapter 13 of the final report, titled "How to Do It? A Different Way of Organizing the Government," the Commission stated: "*We recommend significant changes in the organization of the government. We know that the quality of the people is more important than the quality of the wiring diagrams. Some of the saddest aspects of the 9/11 story are the outstanding efforts of so many individual officials straining, often without success, against the boundaries of the possible. Good people can overcome bad structures. They should not have to.*"[44] The Commission conducted a ten-year assessment of its work in partnership with the Bipartisan Policy Center, which concluded with this lesson: "*Our task is difficult. We must constantly assess our vulnerabilities and anticipate new lines of attack. We have done much, but there is much more to do.*"[45]

A few years after the September 11 attacks, the southeastern United States was hit by one of the most memorable natural disasters in modern history: Hurricane Katrina. In August 2005, Katrina initially landed near Miami, Florida, made its way into

44 *The 9/11 Commission Report,* National Commission on Terrorist Attacks Upon the United States, July 2004, https://govinfo.library.unt.edu/911/report/911Report_Ch13.htm

45 *Tenth Anniversary Report Card: The Status of the 9/11 Commission Recommendations,* Bipartisan Policy Center National Security Preparedness Group report, September 2011, https://bipartisanpolicy.org/download/?file=/wp-content/uploads/2019/03/CommissionRecommendations.pdf

the Gulf of Mexico, strengthened to a Category 5 hurricane, and made landfall as a Category 4 hurricane in Louisiana, impacting Alabama and Mississippi as well.[46] It was one of the strongest storms to hit the United States, with winds estimated at 125 miles per hour. Almost two thousand people died in the storm and its aftermath, while approximately 1.2 million were evacuated, and estimated damage reached as high as $150 billion.[47]

Billions of state and federal dollars were provided to the community, much of which went to residents of New Orleans who were the most significantly impacted by the event.[48] Most of the funding took the form of grants, focusing on housing, unemployment, and cash assistance, with additional monies for infrastructure costs and the rebuilding of the levee system, of which the majority was supported by the US Army Corps of Engineers.[49] As often occurs in natural disasters, the federal agencies distributing the funds included FEMA and the US Department of Housing and Urban Development, through its community development block grants.[50] The SBA made nearly $2.6 billion in low-interest

---

46 *Federal Disaster Assistance After Hurricanes Katrina, Rita, Wilma, Gustav, and Ike*, Congressional Research Service report, February 26, 2019, https://crsreports.congress.gov/product/pdf/R/R43139#:~:text=In%20total%2C%20federal%20agencies%20obligated,assignments%20after%20the%20five%20hurricanes.&text=The%20Small%20Business%20Administration%20approved,Table%2028%20and%20Table%2029)

47 *Federal Disaster Assistance After Hurricanes Katrina, Rita, Wilma, Gustav, and Ike*, Congressional Research Service report

48 *Federal Disaster Assistance After Hurricanes Katrina, Rita, Wilma, Gustav, and Ike*, Congressional Research Service report

49 "The Economic Impact of Hurricane Katrina on its Victims: Evidence from Individual Tax Returns," Tatyana Deryugina, Laura Kawano, and Steven Levitt, American Economic Association, January 2018, https://www.aeaweb.org/content/file?id=6645#:~:text=Many%20resources%20were%20marshalled%20to,flood%20insurance%20payments%20and%20loans

50 "The Economic Impact of Hurricane Katrina on its Victims," Deryugina, Kawano, and Levitt

disaster loans throughout the region, which was accompanied by the presence of agency staff on the ground at identified disaster center locations throughout the region. One special program created for this circumstance was the Road Home Program in New Orleans, where homeowning residents received assistance to rebuild or sell their homes. Between the years 2006 and 2013, about $4.3 billion was given to New Orleans homeowners through this program, alongside millions in flood insurance dollars as part of the National Flood Insurance Program.[51]

While some of the federal government response to Hurricane Katrina was criticized as inefficient, mismanaged, and untimely, there was ultimately massive recovery funding earmarked for this effort. And alongside those funds, one of the lessons of Katrina was that it highlighted the importance of communities and ecosystems for both financial and non-financial support. Sharing technical knowledge, physical and emotional resources—particularly for disadvantaged groups—and the tapping of community networks became critical to the survival of many throughout the region.[52] The lessons learned from Hurricane Katrina also included the need for coordinated and efficient federal response across agencies; advance preparation for a prolonged recovery through thoughtful and tested disaster recovery/business continuity plans, which included substantive support operations and communications across radio, television, internet, and national

51 "The Economic Impact of Hurricane Katrina on its Victims," Deryugina, Kawano, and Levitt

52 "Small Businesses and Government Assistance During COVID-19: Evidence from the PPP in the U.S.," Qingfang Wang and Wei Kang, Sage Journals, April 3, 2023, https://orcid.org/0000-0002-7285-4027; "Lessons Learned from Hurricane Katrina: Preparing Your Institution for a Catastrophic Event," Federal Financial Institutions Examination Council, https://www.ffiec.gov/katrina_lessons.htm

call centers; impact coordination with loan-making financial institutions; identified alternate facilities and infrastructure support; and preparation among key local and regional nonprofits with key centers of influence.[53]

And while both these events were unbelievably horrific with respect to their human toll, the worst national economic downturn since the Great Depression occurred just a few years later, in 2008, which resulted in more than 10 percent unemployment, 30 percent reductions in home prices, and a near 60 percent drop in the S&P 500.[54] The Great Recession is tied to the financial crisis in 2008, which originated from the massive decline in the value of mortgage-backed securities aligned to the systemic defaults of the underlying subprime mortgages.[55] Banks and investment firms held a large portion of these mortgage-backed securities and took enormous losses as pricing fell. These same lenders had also purchased credit default swaps, a kind of insurance policy for bondholders, forcing insurance companies to cover billions of dollars in losses.[56] In order to retain some solvency in the market, bank Bear Stearns was ultimately acquired by JPMorgan Chase, investment bank Lehman Brothers filed for bankruptcy, and the federal government stepped in to provide bailout funds to avoid a domino effect across all of Wall Street. Fannie Mae and Freddie Mac insured several hundred billion dollars in mortgages under September legislation called the Housing and

53 "Lessons Learned from Hurricane Katrina," Federal Financial Institutions Examination Council

54 "A Short History of the Great Recession," Wayne Duggan, Forbes Advisor, NASDAQ, February 22, 2023, https://www.nasdaq.com/articles/a-short-history-of-the-great-recession

55 "A Short History of the Great Recession," Duggan

56 "A Short History of the Great Recession," Duggan

Economic Recovery Act of 2008, and a month later, Congress passed the $700 billion Troubled Asset Relief Program as part of the Emergency Economic Stabilization Act, which served to bail out most of the major banks, auto company General Motors, and insurance company AIG.[57]

The Federal Reserve implemented interest rate cuts, introduced a quantitative easing program, and initiated several new lending programs to support market liquidity.[58] In February 2009, Congress passed the American Recovery and Reinvestment Act, which included tax cuts and monies toward infrastructure education and health care initiatives.[59] There were also additional programs in place to support homeowners through the Homeowner Stability Initiative and the Home Affordable Refinance Program.[60] A significant legislative component of this time period was the passing of the Dodd–Frank Wall Street Reform and Consumer Protection Act in 2010, which established a series of new banking regulations and created the Consumer Financial Protection Bureau.[61] As part of a look back to this time, in the book *First Responders*, former chair of President Obama's Council of Economic Advisers Jason Furman shared several lessons to be considered from the Great Recession, highlighting that discretionary stimulus is impactful in a low-interest rate environment; automatic mechanisms should be in place to account for

57 "A Short History of the Great Recession," Duggan

58 "A Short History of the Great Recession," Duggan

59 "A Short History of the Great Recession," Duggan

60 "A Short History of the Great Recession," Duggan

61 "Paycheck Protection Program Highlights Numerous Oversight Concerns Even as the SBA Makes First Disclosures," Corey Runkel and Rosalind Z. Wiggins, Yale School of Management, July 13, 2020, https://som.yale.edu/blog/paycheck-protection-program-highlights-numerous-oversight-concerns-even-as-the-SBA-makes-first-disclosures

fiscal stimulus fatigue by policymakers; local economic stimulus measures are important; tax cuts in such a crisis may have a significant impact—particularly in underserved communities; and any plan to increase GDP should be aligned to a projected increase in jobs.[62]

The human losses from all these tragedies are heartbreaking, and the economic impacts are almost unimaginable. But we have all now lived through the COVID-19 pandemic, and we all know firsthand the kind of impacts events like these can have on our loved ones, our own health and livelihoods, our communities, and our national economy. And we recognize that while each pandemic is different and the technology to support the responses will undoubtedly be enhanced over time, the assessment of a strategic approach is not only reasonable but critical to inform the next generation of policymakers. With the dire health and economic warnings in February and March 2020, coupled with the actual data that supported these positions, policymakers undoubtedly took steps that combined both proven and creative approaches to defeat an unknown and invisible enemy. While it is, of course, impossible to foresee exactly what the circumstances around a future pandemic or economic crisis will be, this exercise of its most recent equivalent is time well spent.

Not unlike the report that was issued after the September 11 attacks, we now have the time and bandwidth to truly examine the response to the COVID-19 pandemic in a uniquely thorough manner to position ourselves for the crisis yet to come. These

62 *First Responders: Inside the U.S. Strategy for Fighting the 2007–2009 Global Financial Crisis*, Ben S. Bernanke, Timothy F. Geithner, Henry M. Paulson, and Nellie Liang, eds. (Yale University Press, 2020)

efforts, of course, take time, cost money, and will undoubtedly present various bureaucratic challenges and criticisms from both sides of the political aisle, but establishing them in the severe wake of a pandemic that cost so many lives and led to the two largest annual deficits since World War II simply makes sense.[63] As Dr. Osler said, "*The best preparation for tomorrow is to do today's work superbly well.*" And now we turn to the plan for that work.

---

63 *Federal Deficits, Growing Debt, and the Economy in the Wake of COVID-19*, Congressional Research Service report, March 23, 2021, https://crsreports.congress.gov/product/pdf/R/R46729

CHAPTER NINE

A Policy Prescription for the Next Small Business Crisis

No human being is constituted to know the truth, the whole truth and nothing but the truth; and even the best of [people] must be content with fragments, with partial glimpses, never the full fruition.

EVERY CHAPTER THUS FAR HAS begun with the wise words or teachings of Dr. Osler. And hopefully, like the reader, I as the author have learned a few things about policy design in the context of his expertise in diagnosing and treating a condition. As someone who had the tremendous honor to lead the SBA for a time, I recognize that the mere presence of the agency is not a cure-all, but rather it is the intent of the implementing legislation signed into law by President Dwight D. Eisenhower in 1953 and the commitment of the men and women who work there that drive its success to serve the dedicated entrepreneurs and small business owners of our country. What I take away from Dr. Osler's words above is extraordinarily clear. No policymaker will ever be completely positioned to provide the perfect response to a policy problem. There is no university degree, no resume full of expertise, and certainly no crystal ball that will permit such a pure solution. In many ways, the only approach that demonstrates success at any level is recognizing that dilemma, preparing oneself as much as possible for that reality, and making an educated decision on what might be achieved. Study the problem. Know the history. And proceed with the proven techniques and a genuine commitment to help as many people as possible.

But before we embrace what that approach might be in the context of future small business support, we should examine the current state of the patient according to the San Francisco Federal Reserve's 2023 national survey on the state of financing and performance for the small business community.[1] The Federal Reserve found no significant changes from the conditions identified in its previous year's study and highlighted that the impact of the pandemic continued to be substantial on the minds, operations, and financial performance of small business owners.[2] Financing applications dipped somewhat, while funding rates remained steady; however, demographic disparities among younger and minority applicants continued.[3] Half of firms reported decreased revenues, but those that saw some increases were in the fields of childcare, real estate brokers, leisure and hospitality, and retail.[4] While the firms surveyed expect some revenue growth, all expectations were well below pre-pandemic

---

1 *2024 Report on Employer Firms: Findings from the 2023 Small Business Credit Survey*, Federal Reserve Banks report, https://doi.org/10.55350/sbcs-20240307

2 *2024 Report on Employer Firms*, Federal Reserve Banks report

3 *2024 Report on Employer Firms*, Federal Reserve Banks report

4 *2024 Report on Employer Firms*, Federal Reserve Banks report

times.[5] Supply chain and labor market challenges continue to exist, among struggles to keep up with government regulations.[6]

And the hangover from COVID-19-era government funding continues to exist, with over 25 percent of firms still holding debt from EIDL loans and credit card reliance, and almost 60 percent of firms surveyed stating that they relied on some sort of debt instrument during the previous year—most of which went to operating expenses.[7] For those that received loans, most firms that went to banks cited a preexisting relationship, whereas those that were funded by fintechs stressed that their decision was based on the speed of funding.[8] While satisfaction levels at small banks were consistently highest, the satisfaction with online lenders declined from pre-pandemic levels.[9] Many of these businesses provided some qualitative data that shows how small businesses are emerging post-pandemic, including the use of virtual cashiers to remedy their inability to pay a physical worker and the practice of having younger employees also run social media campaigns. But the survey also shows that more businesses are turning to novel financing, such as crowdfunding, while the gap widens between successful and struggling businesses in the wake of rising interest rates.[10]

A notable consistency among the responses to various crises discussed within these pages is that while there are time-tested strategies associated with the approach, the ability for policymakers to be creative is very important. Creating a program from

5 *2024 Report on Employer Firms*, Federal Reserve Banks report

6 *2024 Report on Employer Firms*, Federal Reserve Banks report

7 *2024 Report on Employer Firms*, Federal Reserve Banks report

8 *2024 Report on Employer Firms*, Federal Reserve Banks report

9 *2024 Report on Employer Firms*, Federal Reserve Banks report

10 *2024 Report on Employer Firms*, Federal Reserve Banks report

scratch and in a vacuum is not only difficult but also can be antithetical to the goal, as the negative consequences of the cure could do more damage than the disease itself. That said, the totality of the circumstances will always be different, and with that, policymakers may need to take informed risks on approaches that are reasonably believed to help society. While the study of previous responses to pandemics or negative economic events with common themes is a critical part of any response, policymakers must form these plans with as much real-time data and reliable survey information as possible from the impacted parties. In taking such risks, there will undoubtedly be critics among those devising the response. But embracing transparent and shared responsibilities not only promotes trust among the decision-makers but also provides the public with a clear understanding of the aspirational goals and the potential negative consequences.[11] As such, once decisions are made, a system of consistent and reliable information sharing must be put into place that identifies key categories and provides the results—good or bad—in a sober fashion, with a clear approach to revise tactics where necessary.

To underscore the need for that creativity, governments, corporations, and nonprofit entities often will conduct a disaster recovery exercise to account for the ways in which organizations and their personnel can position themselves in the face of such an unforeseen event. In 2019, a group of fifteen entities, led by the Johns Hopkins Center for Health Security in partnership with the World Economic Forum and the Bill and Melinda Gates

11 "Strategies to Govern Systemic Risks," Stephanie Jacobzone, Charles Baubion, Jack Radisch, Stefan Hochrainer-Stigler, Joanne Linnerooth-Bayer, Wei Liu, Elena Rovenskaya, and Ulf Dieckmann, Organisation for Economic Co-Operation and Development, https://www.oecd-ilibrary.org/sites/e3edb3a4-en/index.html?itemId=/content/component/e3edb3a4-en#endnotea13z2

Foundation, hosted such a simulated event to address cross-functional policies and responsibilities during a potential pandemic event.[12] The results of that event highlighted some key points that any observing policymaker should take to heart in the context of our global economy.

For example, it was demonstrated that cross-country agencies should seek to maintain travel and trade during a pandemic as much as possible. This was cited because this commerce is critical to global economies, and while there may be very good reasons to consider limitations in certain circumstances, fear and uncertainty can unjustifiably lead to the shutting down of businesses, shipping limitations, and supply chain restrictions. And as these events could ultimately impact more advanced economies, the more vulnerable economies will most assuredly face severe consequences in a very short amount of time.[13] While this exercise certainly considered some components of the COVID-19 pandemic that ultimately came to fruition, now that we have a much better understanding of the impact that a modern virus can actually have on contemporary society, a full government after-action report is more than justified.

With respect to PPP, given the options at the time, there is no major disagreement with the good intentions and situational soundness of the program and its approach; however, its most significant criticism emanates from some of its administrative components and execution. While some of these concerns were

12 "Tabletop Exercise Event 201," Johns Hopkins Bloomberg School of Public Health Center for Health Security, October 18, 2019, https://centerforhealthsecurity.org/our-work/tabletop-exercises/event-201-pandemic-tabletop-exercise

13 "Tabletop Exercise Event 201," Johns Hopkins Bloomberg School of Public Health Center for Health Security

mitigated or remedied over time, I believe all would agree that improvements can be made. Notwithstanding the facts that the program was built so quickly, involved such a significant amount of money, and was dependent on so many government and private sector actors, its administration helped many businesses and secured millions of jobs. However, as we have explored, developing the response to the next pandemic from an informed foundation is critical. With that in mind, I have broken down the most frequently identified program criticisms/symptoms of the PPP and offer a possible policy prescription to address that symptom, along with the appropriate risk mitigation protocol where appropriate. These "symptoms" are set forth in three categories: (1) prioritizing the target market and programs for economic support, (2) operational program design and infrastructure enhancements, and (3) lender engagement. An examination of the policy prescriptions to administer before the next pandemic will hopefully serve as the basis for a meaningful bipartisan policy conversation on this important issue for our country.

1. PRIORITIZING TARGET MARKET AND PROGRAMS FOR ECONOMIC SUPPORT

In a more traditional recession, access to capital is the critical lever, as was seen in the Great Recession and other major crises. While this remains very important in a pandemic-driven recession, given the public health constraints, the approach must be somewhat different. As such, the PPP was designed to ensure that small business employees could remain in those roles, thereby allowing them to pay their bills, retain their health insurance, and spend as consumers to support the larger economy. Given the variety of employees, industry sectors, and various socioeconomic conditions, prioritizing the appropriate target market for this support will be critical in preparation for the next pandemic.

Program Symptom: Concentration of Design on Job Retention and Small Business Support

Given the need for access to current impact data and viable policy options for small businesses and their employees during such a difficult period, there are a series of advance steps that can be considered—and perhaps acted upon—to augment the program design to further support the resilience of these communities.

Policy Prescription

- Coordinate with private sector employee payroll data providers to determine how anonymized data sets from existing or specialized real-time reports could enhance visibility into market trends in unemployment to ensure that the impact of any envisioned program is consistent with the policy underpinnings, with the flexibility to revise focus as industry trends modify.
- Commit to enhancing technologies of all state unemployment insurance systems to give policymakers a viable robust framework to pair with any future PPP/ stimulus action. Like the payroll approach above, this effort could also generate anonymized data sharing, centralized reporting, and program modification as

situations require—noting that privacy protections would be critical.

- Determine the possibility of regional pilots for short-term work models for states that currently have this in place, comparable to the approach in Europe that steadied unemployment by focusing on more viable industries. If deemed effective, policymakers could assess how the impact of this approach would affect any additional targeted stimulus plan. (Note: This methodology could include government-subsidized apprenticeship programs—as seen in Europe—for these same industries to reskill workers or employ graduating students or previously unemployed individuals.)
- Consider if the federal government wants to explore which businesses would be deemed healthy enough or industry critical to participate in a PPP-like program. While use of such a standard presents a difficult policy issue, including appropriate taxpayer stewardship and the traditional moral hazard questions, viability was an approach that was incorporated into European models, particularly in the Recovery Period of the COVID-19 pandemic.
- Examine a tiered/targeted model that releases stimulus funding according to the revenue replacement need for the particular business, beginning with smaller amounts to smaller firms to stabilize them and then including larger firms as appropriate (within the sub-five-hundred-person limit). While the management of such an approach could be chal-

lenging, it would provide for a lens of real-time need, allowing for additional distributions over the course of the pandemic, which also would also serve as a data-gathering source for policymakers.

Program Symptom: Lack of a Material Macroeconomic Needs Assessment by Congress Prior to PPP Passage

As has been discussed, the bipartisan nature of such a crisis did, in fact, assist in the development and passage of the PPP, the CARES Act, and its progeny legislation. And of course, the expedited timing of the effort made it difficult, if not impossible, for the appropriators to conduct a robust needs assessment.

Policy Prescription

- Establish a bipartisan congressional review board that concentrates on gaming out various pandemic scenarios to determine the most critical economic and industry needs in advance—given the conditions set forth in a particular simulation. Results should be transparent, and industry associations should be positioned to provide substantive feedback so that policymakers have their input for the larger economic ecosystem and policy clarity in the public square. While processes can be informed by the work of the 9/11 Commission, the ultimate work product should include a variety of scenarios to be considered and include country, state, and local disaster recovery and business continuity plans, as well as a step-by-step playbook for local communities to help them do the same in advance of an actual pandemic scenario. Results from this review should include what their implementation plan would be with their most prominent industries, including input from representative small business owners, chambers of commerce, and state workforce boards. Key trade association participants to assist in coordinating this work would include but certainly not be limited to groups like the National Governors Association, the National League of Cities, and the National Association of Counties. (Note: This work may be governed by the Federal Advisory Committee Act.)

- Such an assessment would also be helpful when establishing companion programs, such as EIDL, to determine if agency technology and operations are able to handle that kind of mandate or if it would be better supervised by a different part of the government.

Program Symptom: Access by Non-Qualifying Larger Businesses

While many of the businesses that applied for PPP genuinely needed the funds, there were some that did not or that could have reasonably obtained funding through some other manageable market-based circumstances. As part of the program, Congress waived the SBA "affiliation" and "credit elsewhere" rules, which enabled funding requests from subsidiaries, certain franchisees, and companies that may have had access to various levels of public market, private equity, or venture capital investment, many of which would not have had traditional access to SBA's financial support. This symptom caused program confusion and several scenarios where loans were made and then returned by parties.

Policy Prescription

- Maintain the express guidance that the SBA ultimately provided to explicitly make it clear that this type of company access was not only the intent of the program but also that there was an affirmative obligation on the potential borrower to assess this and certify accordingly. While policymakers may want to consider adjusting the small business definition ceiling to a number below the traditional five-hundred-employee threshold for this type of emergency program, at a minimum, the established guidance should be repeated in any future program rollout. In fact, once the issue of public companies taking PPP funds was determined, government leadership made the above guidance available and made cabinet-level public statements about the government's intent to prosecute offenders. To ensure that there is sufficient public notice of this message and associated actions in a future situation, government officials should not only make public remarks about this concern early on but also determine whether any emergency legislation requires additional civil or criminal authorities to effectively deter bad actors.

Program Symptom: Program Accounting for Independent Contractors, Gig Workers, and the New Workforce Economy

While COVID-19-era programs ultimately allowed for full access by independent contractors and gig workers, an increase in technology innovation and the opportunity to establish more virtually based companies will likely lead to a significant spike in these populations in any future pandemic. While the unemployment insurance component can certainly play a role, there will need to be a plan in place to account for the size of this new workforce.

Policy Prescription

- Consider including this population in a piloted support program that is specific to sole proprietorships and single member limited liability companies. While access to unemployment insurance may suffice, these workers and these companies experienced unique challenges that should be thought through in advance of the next pandemic event. As is discussed elsewhere in this section, if a short-term work pilot is considered by the states, this group may be a ready-made population for that piloted engagement.

Program Symptom: PPP Benefited the Creditors of Borrowers More than the Actual Borrowers

Some critics have shared that the PPP may have provided more benefit to the creditors of the small businesses than to their employees, citing operational payments made from the administrative portion of the loans to third parties, such as landlords and banks with which prior debt was held. While there may be technical merit to this point, these were real and necessary payments for a business to function and remain viable to employ workers, and there is certainly macroeconomic benefit from this spending.

Policy Prescription

- Allow the practice of payments to creditors to continue so that businesses remain viable and can maintain a workplace for employees to be sustained beyond the end of the pandemic period. An assessment should be conducted as to whether the allowable percentages during PPP were in fact the right amounts to be spent on reasonable operational expenses, as that analysis may have had additional meaningful benefits to businesses, particularly those that may have closed or were forced to declare bankruptcy due to pandemic conditions.

2. OPERATIONAL PROGRAMS AND INFRASTRUCTURE ENHANCEMENT

While the intent of the PPP was to get funds into the hands of the American workers and keep them connected to their employer, there was significant internal infrastructure that was developed initially at the SBA and then within the lenders themselves to be able to accept applications, make funds available, and institute the loan forgiveness process. This section will examine how to provide a foundational model in advance of the next pandemic.

<u>Program Symptom</u>: All-of-Government Disaster Preparation Program

As discussed above, it is not uncommon for private sector companies and certain government agencies to conduct business continuity/disaster planning tabletop exercises, where the organization is faced with a series of spontaneous internal and external challenges to assess their vulnerabilities. Given that many of these activities are limited to that organization, the interdependencies—particularly for governments—are not able to be properly pressure-tested and vetted for performance. The inability to determine if and how an important paper action plan truly meets its objectives can and will cause cascading consequences. And while there are individual agency plans that can be used for foundational support—particularly from the public health perspective—strict economic protocols are not necessarily as detailed in the context of potential crisis scenarios. Further, while certain oversight and review committees have been instituted, their efforts have become increasingly political in nature, which can often blur the areas of blame and progress.

Policy Prescription

- Plan an all-of-government tabletop exercise on the topic of a pandemic that includes representatives from various executive agencies, Congress, governors' staffs, and relevant private sector participants (e.g., lenders, small businesses, universities, and trade associations). This activity could be overseen by a bipartisan congressional review committee and perhaps administratively managed by the US Health and Human Services' Administration for Strategic Preparedness and Response (ASPR), with economic experts detailed to support as necessary. It should be robust in nature, well-planned, and documented, and the results should be available to the public.

Program Symptom: Preparation for Crisis Legislation/Political Bipartisanship

Political disfunction is certainly an issue that all Americans understand and appreciate; however, the legitimate debate of mutual policy priorities in an emergency circumstance may need to occur on an expedited basis to maximize the impact of the ultimate legislation. While the White House, Senate, and House leadership will, of course, be critical to streamline and advance efforts, additional preparation may be helpful.

Policy Prescription

- Provide a framework for Congress to take note of its success during the passage of the CARES Act and employ a future strategy that accounts for certain pre-agreed-upon legislative components for any future event. Pieces of this strategy may already be available as part of the textbook approach, such as access to a Federal Reserve facility for certain businesses; however, gaming out priorities could save significant delays in a true time of need. This work, along with much of what is discussed herein, could be led by a bipartisan congressional review committee, which could also incorporate retired policymakers, like the 9/11 Commission.

- Consider whether there is an appetite for any international institution (e.g., the World Bank or International Monetary Fund) to assist in fiscal policy best practices or impact coordination on multinational firms that have cross-country industry relevance.

Program Symptom: Need for Administrative Clarity and Program Communication

The most frequent complaint of the PPP from both borrowers and lenders was a lack of administrative clarity. Not surprisingly, the difficulty here was that the Treasury and SBA staff had to develop the written guidance in real time, making changes in response to operational feedback while the program was already in flight.

Policy Prescription

- Develop advance draft rules and program guidance in coordination with career agency personnel, representative small businesses of varying sizes, and a representative group of lenders, including but not limited to large and small banks, credit unions, MDIs, CDFIs, program-approved fintechs, and farm credit lenders. Recognizing that portions of these guidelines may need to change based on the type of crisis, if aligned with the bipartisan legislative initiative discussed herein, agency staff can use public templates as needed. (Note:

These draft rules and guidance must endeavor to be easy to understand and focus on a variety of topics, including but not limited to guidance around qualifying businesses, documents required, loan forgiveness processes, and lender safe harbor provisions.)

- Appoint a single agency point of contact who is as senior as possible and knowledgeable on the final programs to conduct very regular press briefings across all media vehicles, which should include how borrowers can utilize the process, program tutorials, and updates to the public on any changes to the programs.

Program Symptom: Access by Fraudulent Actors

As discussed herein, there has been and there will very likely continue to be fraud found within the program—the size of which is still to be determined. The investigations of the SBA Office of the Inspector General are ongoing, and the law enforcement community will bring cases accordingly. That said, while it was universally understood that any such program would likely have to endure some level of fraud, to guard against this as much as possible in the future, the SBA needs to take specific steps that will protect against, publicly deter, and identify fraudulent loan activities as early as possible.

Policy Prescription

- Conduct a full post-PPP risk assessment of each operational process from application through forgiveness to ensure all internal protocols are documented, as well as identify if available technologies need to be purchased from third parties to address any vulnerabilities for future programs. Given organizations like GAO's concern over self-certification as a fraud factor, conduct a deep dive as to whether the utility of this approach can be reasonably mitigated while still supporting the mission and speed required to effectuate such an initiative. Additional areas of concern represented by the SBA OIG include an assessment of accounts that presented hold codes flagged for fraud, duplication of employer identification numbers, changes in deposit accounts of borrowers, affiliated hotline complaints, and/or suspicious physical and email addresses. Some additional services to be considered to mitigate fraudulent activities include a geolocation analysis for internet protocol addresses associated with borrower applications and nonpayment/default or lack of application for loan forgiveness.

- Engage with Congress and/or the bipartisan congressional review committee to determine whether additional legislative language is needed to streamline investigations and civil and criminal actions.
- Ensure there is consistent external messaging that expresses that fraud protocols are in place and violators will be pursued, coupled with the necessary resources from Congress to appropriately fund investigations and prosecutions.

- Safeguard that all agency auditing standards are consistent with professional standards and industry capabilities, including meaningful sample sizes of average dollar loan thresholds.

Program Symptom: Assessing the Overall Approach in the Context of a Rescue Period and Recovery Period

Across Europe, many countries approached the first few months of the COVID-19 pandemic as a Rescue Period, which was heavily weighted toward grants and loans to small businesses; then, after that, the approach embraced a Recovery Period mindset. As such, various financial products became available and small businesses adapted accordingly. This resulted in many countries seeing relatively steady unemployment numbers from before March 2020.

Policy Prescription

- Assess the economic impact of the PPP loan tranches to determine if there is a reasonable delineation to employ a two-tiered approach that incorporates a Rescue Period earlier and then a Recovery Period. Once completed, determine if a more holistic way of addressing job retention and economic challenges can be done through framework, including the introduction of additional financial products in the Recovery Period, as was seen in other parts of the world, such as factoring, tax deferrals, alternative finance vehicles, public-private partnerships, cost reductions, labor readiness programs, crowdfunding, and investments in innovation.

- Consider the support for and incubation of new and existing state infrastructure banks to determine if they could serve as complimentary organizations to the federal government's pandemic response, including their ability to administer block grants, public-private community investment funds, and different financial products with the local focus of a state's needs, industries, workforce, and geographies.

Program Symptom: Program Alignment with Support Infrastructure for State and Local Economies

One of the most critical lessons of these types of crisis situations is the importance of local community engagement to advance the small business ecosystem. In a national emergency, governors, mayors, and local officials often look to the federal government to provide answers. Preparing appropriate models in advance now will pay significant dividends in the future.

Policy Prescription

- Organize SBA and its resource partners, (e.g., SBDCs, SCORE, Women's Business Centers, Veterans Business Outreach Centers) to convene and facilitate a meaningful best practices framework that can be duplicated through its local district offices across all communities and includes:

  - coordination of Fortune 500 corporate responsibility efforts for non-financial/technical assistance support for city/state ecosystems;
  - state workforce board action plans for reskilling employees; and
  - engagement with critical local nonprofits and the religious communities that were able to access the PPP and traditionally provide significant resources and information to their congregations, including access to government resources, job fairs, and mental health support for workers and entrepreneurs.
- Provide local ecosystems with a blueprint of innovative ways to deregulate and deliver government and private sector services during pandemics (e.g., Miami data coordination with credit card consortia, regulatory reviews, and efficient business licensing processes) and limit/suspend nonessential regulatory hurdles to allow small businesses to operate, innovate, and serve customers.

3. LENDER ENGAGEMENT

In the massive public-private partnership that was the PPP, the lending community was the key partner in distributing funds to the small businesses. Serving in that role, this diverse ecosystem of national, state, community, and digital lenders must have a clarity of process so that they know what they are being asked to do, how they will implement the necessary operations, and that their performance will then be reviewed accordingly. While all the government assessments and rule-writing processes discussed within these recommendations will be very beneficial to this effort, there are additional steps that could be considered.

<u>Program Symptom</u>: Banks Prioritizing Preexisting Relationships and Funding on a First-Come-First-Served Basis

Many banks were criticized during the PPP rollout among claims that they were prioritizing their clients over other PPP applicants. As was previously discussed, banks were directed to fund on a first-come-first-served basis, reportedly turning much of their attention to existing clients. Certainly, the fact that they had already completed fraud checks on their clients meant that loans could be processed faster to meet the government's goal of distribution; however, there were public criticisms associated with these actions. Whereas it has also been posited that a more robust congressional appropriation at the outset could have slowed the concern that the PPP funds would have been exhausted so quickly, the issue at hand is determining how all impacted small businesses can more efficiently access the traditional banking system during such a crisis. And while certain other recommendations herein tend to be more responsive to that issue, there are some steps that can immediately address the prioritization concern.

Policy Prescription

- Provide written clarity to lenders as to whether they should/should not prioritize preexisting customers to distribute funds faster, or if they should take a different approach to address the appropriate policy concern of access. If directing banks to take a certain approach, the government must be very clear about what that approach is and how it should be implemented; and banks must have realistic incentives to be able to operationalize any such program, including very public clarity on safe harbor from regulatory scrutiny or private legal action, as may be appropriate.

- Determine and publicize any policy priorities beyond speed, if applicable, to ensure that lenders understand and can operationalize those policy goals for distribution, including any necessary clarity around required geographic distributions, or within underserved areas via existing benchmarks such as HUBZone maps or census data.
- Ensure that lenders have mandates that align with their current processes as much as possible (e.g., using IRS forms for loans as opposed to payroll statements) in order to avoid either a human or technology learning curve where possible. As such, incorporating lender engagement in the draft rule writing process will allow for pre-identifiable operational efficiencies for the lender, with the goal of a simpler and streamlined application process.

Program Symptom: Role of Financial Technology Firms

Many fintechs entered the ranks of SBA lenders during the PPP. While they played a significant role in distributing funds, particularly to many underserved communities, there were significant concerns around the levels of allegedly fraudulent loans that came through that pipeline. The reality is that fintechs will continue to be a part of the small business lending ecosystem, and if overseen appropriately, can increase access to capital for entrepreneurs.

Policy Prescription

- Mandate that any fintech involved in small business lending maintains appropriate internal controls and audit functionality commensurate with the risk they pose.
- Establish more robust funding for more SBA oversight resources either through government appropriations or through fees paid by licensed entities, as is done by other agencies.

Program Symptom: Underserved Communities and the Role of Community-Based Lenders

While community-based lenders (e.g., small and community banks, MDIs, CDFIs, and certain credit unions) played an important role in distributing PPP dollars, they were particularly impactful in supporting underserved communities that either did not have access to, or chose not to engage in, other parts of the banking system. The pandemic demonstrated that those communities that were economically vulnerable prior to the pandemic became much more exposed once it started.

Policy Prescription

- Ensure that representatives from these community lenders are at the drafting table for future planning discussions and tabletop exercises testing potential rules, regulations, and operational processes in order to account for any identified areas of concern. Such a partnership could facilitate real-time information sharing and policy changes to a future program that can seek to balance speed and access.
- Engage with key financial agency committees (e.g., the Financial Literacy Education Committee at the Treasury Department) and nonprofit/private sector partners to advance a business support curriculum—preferably aligned with states and counties that can be tailored to a particular community. Use these resources as communication channels for program updates.
- Determine whether community lender funding set-asides or exclusive lending windows should be periodic throughout the pandemic.
- Promote state programs that encourage community lenders to participate in programs that pair government funds with private capital to be leveraged for lending throughout particular states and regions (e.g., Southern Opportunity and Resilience Fund).

CONCLUSION

Soap and water and common sense are the best disinfectants.

THE DISCUSSION OVER THE COURSE of this book has gone from the lecture halls of Johns Hopkins and Oxford medical schools to the US Capitol building, to the Oval Office of the White House, and to countries all around the globe. There have been examinations of world-changing events, the development of innovative technologies, and the application of cutting-edge enterprise risk protocols. And while the answer to developing a stronger defense against economic contagion caused by a pandemic virus is quite complicated, we must start somewhere in fighting off the possible adversary.

And taking a final lesson from Dr. Osler that the simple act of washing your hands is still the best way to avoid viruses, you have embraced the simple act of reading this book. Handwashing alone will likely not guard against the next pandemic, just as this book alone will not serve as the final word on economic responses to that event. However, it is an important first step in the conversation that will hopefully lead to both public and private sector actions to study these issues and provide the American people with the clarity and reassurance that the next time this happens, we will have learned from our previous experience and be ready to address the challenge.

Dr. Osler believed that the natural tendency of disease is recovery, provided that the proper administration of care was present. And while all arcs of all diseases, tragic events, and economic crises are not always predictable, there is a rough policy framework that was introduced to me by noted Osler historian Dr. Charles Bryan. He shared a paradigm set forth by historian of medicine and science Charles Rosenberg that theorizes that pandemics often unfold as a four-act play. The first act tends to focus on the recognition of a problem where public officials tend to downplay its impact. After cases accumulate, the next act highlights something of a randomness of the contagion, its impact on highly vulnerable individuals, the demands on the scientific community, and the introduction of all kinds of qualified and unqualified theories alike. The third act features government intervention, including the need, the impact, and the costs, as well as the concept of the responsibilities of the citizenry. As one might imagine, in the final act, the disease begins to subside and academics wrangle over the history, the health impacts, and the ethics of the events that have taken place. Rosenberg's concept is prescient in that we now find ourselves somewhere in that fourth act, and we will have to wait to see just how this play ends and how we recover before the next inevitable crisis.

But until then, I know I will remain hopeful that committed policymakers, entrepreneurs, and the many passionate supporters of small businesses across America will continue to advocate on behalf of small businesses in both the good times and in the challenging periods as well. And while a piece of government legislation is not always the best place to look for inspiring poetic prose, I believe that these words may be an exception:

The essence of the American economic system of private enterprise is free competition. Only through full and free competition can free markets, free entry into business, and opportunities for the expression and growth of personal initiative and individual judgment be assured. The preservation and expansion of such competition is basic not only to the economic well-being but to the security of this Nation. Such security and well-being cannot be realized unless the actual and potential capacity of small business is encouraged and developed.

—Preface to the US Small Business Act of 1953

ACKNOWLEDGMENTS

As I HAVE PREVIOUSLY WORKED at the SBA and then within the White House during the COVID-19 pandemic, this writing has meant quite a bit to me to ensure that there is a resource for policymakers to turn to in the next crisis, recession, or significant economic event.

I begin by thanking two groups of people—the pandemic frontline health care workers, doctors, and nurses; and the small business owners that supported each other and their communities throughout the entire crisis. Your collective commitment to your fellow Americans and your country was nothing short of heroic.

Next, while I am very appreciative of my friend Larry Kudlow writing the foreword to this book, both I and the American people will always be profoundly grateful for his steady leadership during the pandemic.

I would also like to thank my former colleagues from the US Small Business Administration, the US Department of the Treasury, and the White House, with particular thanks to SBA Administrator Linda McMahon for the opportunity to serve the agency, as well as the insights and advice of Chair of the Council of Economic Advisers Kevin Hassett, Assistant Treasury

Secretary for Economic Policy Michael Faulkender, Acting SBA Associate Administrator for Capital Access Bill Briggs, and Deputy Director of the National Economic Council Andrew Olmem, who also serves as my coauthor on a related PPP case study at Harvard. Along with these individuals, I must specifically recognize the incredible career staff at the SBA who worked so tirelessly alongside many committed lenders to advance small business programs during the entirety of the pandemic.

The development of this book has benefited from the thoughtful engagement of numerous wonderful people, many of whom are affiliated with the Harvard Kennedy School's Mossavar-Rahmani Center for Business and Government (M-RCBG). Having served there as a Senior Fellow from 2023 to 2024, I was among a very supportive environment that truly nurtured this research. Here, I must begin by acknowledging Joseph McCarthy and Dana Thompson, both of whom are fellow alums of Gonzaga High School (Washington, DC) who encouraged me to participate in the M-RCBG program. I am also very appreciative to the leadership of M-RCBG: Professors Richard Zeckhauser and John Haigh, as well as colleagues Dan Murphy, Susan Gill, and Claire Byrne, all of whom shepherd this unique program in a very impactful way.

I would also like to thank many of the faculty at the Harvard Kennedy School who were engaged in the review and feedback associated with this work, particularly my faculty adviser, Professor Jason Furman. I certainly could not have sharpened this analysis without all the insights from the other Senior Fellows in the program, as their expertise was so incredibly helpful to my ongoing work. Further, the Harvard Kennedy School is fortunate to have so many talented students, and I was also the beneficiary of this talent, as the work of my research assistant Samya Mishra was invaluable to building out the framework and digging into the PPP, the global models, and much of the other financial services components of this work.

There were also a number of Dr. Osler scholars who were so generous with their time and contributions, namely Dr. Mary Hague-Yearl, Dr. Rolando Del Maestro, and Dr. Charles Bryan. Along with these folks, I must extend my gratitude to others for their valuable input, including Mary McAndrews, Christopher Gergen, and James Ballantine, as well Luz Urrutia and my colleagues at Accion Opportunity Fund, who alongside many other community institutions, did so much to support underserved communities during the pandemic.

Finally, I would like to thank my wonderful wife, Amanda, and the rest of my family for all their love and support during the production of this book.

ABOUT THE AUTHOR

Chris Pilkerton is the former Acting Administrator and General Counsel of the US Small Business Administration, and White House Senior Policy Advisor. His career has included being an Assistant District Attorney in Manhattan, Senior Counsel at the US Securities and Exchange Commission, Compliance Director at JP Morgan Chase, and an executive with the leading community development financial institution focused on small businesses. He has been a Senior Fellow at the Harvard University Kennedy School of Government and an Executive in Residence at both the Georgetown University McDonough School of Business and the Johns Hopkins University Carey Business School. He was a Fulbright Teaching Scholar and holds an MPA from Columbia University, a JD from Catholic University of America, and a BA from Fairfield University. His previous titles include *Underserved: Harnessing the Principles of Lincoln's Vision for Reconstruction for Today's Forgotten Communities* and *Courses: A Menu for Public Policy with Chef James Beard and Senator J. William Fulbright.*

www.ingramcontent.com/pod-product-compliance
Ingram Content Group UK Ltd.
Pitfield, Milton Keynes, MK11 3LW, UK
UKHW021651190726
13853UKWH00001B/199

9 798888 456989